THE COOKBOOK IN SUPPORT OF THE UNITED NATIONS

FOR PEOPLE & PLANET

Published by Familius LLC, www.familius.com
PO Box 1249, Reedley, CA 93654

Familius books are available at special discounts for bulk purchases, whether for sales promotions or for
family or corporate use. For more information, contact Familius Sales at orders@familius.com.

Library of Congress Control Number: 2021937157

Print ISBN 978-1-64170-584-4
Ebook ISBN 978-1-64170-598-1
FE 978-1-64170-612-4
KF 978-1-64170-626-1

Printed in China using FSC® Certified materials

Contributor illustrations by Deni Pramadita
Edited by Lauren Salkeld, Lindsay Sandberg, Peg Sandkam, and Sarah Echard
Cover and book design by Brooke Jorden

10 9 8 7 6 5 4 3 2 1

First Edition

UNDER THE DIRECTION OF EARLENE CRUZ AT KITCHEN CONNECTION

THE COOKBOOK IN SUPPORT OF THE UNITED NATIONS

FOR PEOPLE & PLANET

75 Sustainable International Recipes from
Chefs, Farmers & Indigenous Communities

with **KIMBAL MUSK,
AMBASSADOR HANS HOOGEVEEN,**

& Chefs Manal Al Alem, José Andrés, Daniel Boulud,
Massimo Bottura, Rosalia Chay Chuc, Virgilio Martínez,
Grace Ramirez, Pierre Thiam & Andrew Zimmern

This book is dedicated to our planet,
for the way that it relentlessly nourishes us.

ACKNOWLEDGMENTS

With special thanks to Ambassador Hans Hoogeveen,
without whom this project would not have seen the light of day.

IT COULD NOT HAVE BEEN MADE POSSIBLE WITHOUT:

Principal Editor and Managing Director: Earlene Cruz
Supervisors: Hawa Diallo and Zitouni Ould Dada
Editor: Lauren Salkeld
Administrative Assistant: Angelina Abbott
Photographer: Lara Ferroni
Carbon Analyst: Leigh Anne Statuto
Nutritional Analyst: Charlotte Shron
Recipe Analyst: Lucia Albero
Supporting Authors: Sara Bond and Emily M. Hoey

AUTHOR CONTRIBUTORS:

The Food System: Earlene Cruz, Kitchen Connection | Hawa Diallo, UN Department of Global Communications | Section on Indigenous Food Systems by: Mariana Estrada, Yon Fernández de Larrinoa, Ida Strømsø, Food and Agriculture Organization of the United Nations
Biodiversity: Sara Bond, Earlene Cruz, Kitchen Connection
Sustainable Consumption: Sara Farley and John de la Parra, Rockefeller Foundation
Food & Climate Change: Zitouni Ould Dada, Food and Agriculture Organization of the United Nations
Reducing Food Waste: Ryan Brown, Glenda Cabralcalzuola, Francesca Gianfelici, Rosa Rolle, Food and Agriculture Organization of the United Nations

SUPPORTERS:

Juan Alzate, Jessica Bihuniak, Edward Bogart, Joseph Karl Corcoran, Swati Dave, Giulia DeCastro, Olivia Diaz, Niamh Holland Essoh, Alejandro Espinoza, Ethan Frisch, Victoria Gorelik, Alejandra Gutierrez, Johnathan Homan, Liva Kaugure, Olav Kjørven, Mira Kleist, Brian Matias, Veronica Matias, Emilie McGlone, Charles McNeill, Julie Murphy, Sandra Noonan, Tolu Olubunmi, Pooja Premchandran, Krishnendu Ray, Maximilian Sköries, Simen Sletsjøe, Zoja Stojanovic, Ida Strømsø, Brian Thomson, Satya Tripathi, Rosleny Ubiñas, Anita Yan, Luisa Volpe, Kathrin Wessenberg

EAT Foundation
Global Alliance for Climate Smart Agriculture
International Fund for Agricultural Development
Rockefeller Foundation
World Food Forum

SPONSORS:

The Kingdom of the Netherlands
Whole Foods Market
The Food and Agriculture Organization of the United Nations

And of course, all of our contributors and their teams: the chefs, farmers, indigenous communities, recipe testers and members of civil society who came together to stand for a better food system.

CONTENTS

III. Sustainable Consumption | 95

IV. Food & Climate Change | 133

V. Reducing Food Waste | 175

Components of Our Food | 213

Nutrition Labeling Methodology | 217

Recipe Nutrition Information | 219

FOREWORD BY
Kimbal Musk

I've never met someone who hasn't experienced the magic of a good meal. Whether it's a family recipe that tastes like home or a new ingredient that smells like adventure, bringing food to the table is what brings us all together. But bringing real food to people—food that you trust to nourish your community, feed the hands that grew it and preserve the world around you—is the opportunity of our generation. Real food is for everyone. My mother is a registered dietitian-nutritionist and passed down this belief to our family with every fistful of fresh greens she harvested from our garden.

I graduated from cooking school in New York City right before the September 11th terrorist attacks and was able to prepare meals for the firefighters working to piece the city back together. I chopped thousands of potatoes in a partially destroyed restaurant and drove an ATV carrying dinners past giant piles of melting metal . . . I'll never forget the smell. The firefighters, exhausted from their search to find anyone still alive, changed when we served them: Conversation got louder. They reconnected with each other. Their eyes came back to life. This is when I realized that food can do more than nourish: it can heal.

I opened my first two restaurants shortly after, but healing and food connected for me a second time when I flipped off a tube during a 2010 skiing trip and broke my neck. As I lay recovering, I realized I had an opportunity to restart the way I approached spreading my message. I could lead with velocity and conviction in pursuit of the change I wanted to see—qualities demonstrated by my brother, Elon.

I grew my restaurant group, The Kitchen. I cofounded Big Green, a nonprofit organization that believes growing food changes lives and has built hundreds of outdoor classrooms at schools across America and seeks to empower and uplift the people on the frontlines of growing food. I cofounded Square Roots, an urban farming company. What all three organizations have shown me is that no single approach or company can solve the vast food systems challenges we face. Instead, we need to work together—and it starts with rewriting the norms in our own homes and in our own communities.

As you will learn in this book, biodiversity is slipping through our fingers. Our actions are destroying the complex web of life on our planet—through overconsumption, conversion of natural land to industrial agricultural land and climate change. Here's good news: We already have enough agricultural land to feed everyone on the planet. There is no reason to sacrifice any more forests or irreplaceable natural resources. Research proves that shifting to more sustainable diets can do more than improve our health—it can help us save the planet.

At home and in my restaurants, I know that flavor-filled, energizing, sustainably produced food is a joy to prepare, eat and share with others. That is what led me to this cookbook. This book is more than ingredient lists and gorgeous photography—it tells the stories of people. People who make choices every day about what they put on their plates and in their bodies. People like you and me.

I believe in this book. I believe in the beauty and honesty of its contributors, the power of its information, the nourishing qualities of its recipes and the impact that it will have within the hearts of its readers. Will you join me?

Kimbal Musk
Restaurateur, Chef, Entrepreneur

INTRODUCTION BY
Ambassador Hans Hoogeveen,
The Netherlands

Dear Culinary Enthusiast,

Our world is changing quickly around us. Innovations spring up daily like seedlings in spring, but this expansion is not without consequence: despite our progress, more than 700 million people live in hunger; 2 billion do not have access to safe, affordable and nutritious food; and 1.6 billion suffer from nutrition-related diseases. The dots don't connect: one-third of food produced globally is wasted, but children are still hungry? We can produce more food than ever, but biodiversity and amounts of arable land are decreasing? We can fly over the Pacific Ocean in a day, but viruses can derail our supply chain and leave communities vulnerable? To speak plainly, the shortcomings of our global food system have been laid bare.

Thankfully, we have a roadmap to a more just and sustainable future. The United Nations has developed a series of 17 Sustainable Development Goals: objectives that, if reached, can help us end poverty, protect the planet and ensure that all people enjoy peace and prosperity. These detailed calls to action provide a framework and direction—but we must act quickly and boldly if the Goals are to be achieved.

If you have been waiting for an invitation to bring sustainable food practices into your home, consider this cookbook addressed to you. We are truly nations, united; we struggle and succeed together. Our triumph over global hunger will belong to all of us and requires all of us in its pursuit.

As an Ambassador/Permanent Representative of the Kingdom of the Netherlands to the UN Organizations for Food and Agriculture, it is my life's work to find concrete solutions for many of these challenges. We are constantly seeking ways to improve the food system, like making agriculture more climate-friendly, minimizing food loss and providing more nutritious food for all.

I am motivated by our youth. I hope to leave them with the planet and global community that they deserve—not one that will greet them with challenges and inequity. Their fresh ideas, admirable determination and unquenchable hope for a brighter future continue to inspire my work. I am certain that today's young people will become truly global citizens and the final champions for peace and food security.

Our youth teach us that in unity, there is strength. That strength is why I am supportive of initiatives like the Kitchen Connection Alliance, a space that empowers *everyone* to be part of positive change. The Kitchen Connection Alliance connects everyday citizens to the global food system through food and its culture. It welcomes organizations and individuals from all backgrounds and specialties to gather around our collective table over a hot plate of food, to participate in the political, economic and social conversations that shape our lives.

I firmly believe in the power of food to connect us, as it did when I was introduced to the founder of the Kitchen Connection Alliance, Earlene Cruz. Earlene embodies the bravery, tenacity and thoughtfulness that the food system needs to serve all people, and this cookbook could not have happened without her perseverance. I hope you enjoy the cuisines, cultures and stories told within these pages, and that the recipes transport you from your kitchen to a Cambodian pepper farm or the Italian countryside.

The Nutrition and Carbon Calculations in the book add another layer of awareness. Can our food choices celebrate our history while supporting human and planetary health? These 75 delicious recipes prove that we can, and I hope that we can continue to leverage tools like these to guide our families, communities and nations towards sustainable choices.

Let us take to the farm, field, market or kitchen with newfound delight and determination. Let us break bread, build bonds and set lofty goals. Let us step back and gaze in wonderment at the planet we are lucky enough to inhabit and the people who make it worth living upon. With hearts full, let us take on our part to make this world the best it can be.

> "If you realize you are only a violin, you can open yourself up to the world by playing your role in the concert."
>
> Jacques Yves Cousteau

Dr. Hans Hoogeveen
Ambassador/Permanent Representative of
the Kingdom of the Netherlands to the Rome-based
UN Organizations for Food and Agriculture

INTRODUCTION BY
Earlene Cruz,
Kitchen Connection

As children of restaurateurs often do, I wanted a different path for myself.

Growing up, the restaurant that my family ran was my life, literally and figuratively feeding me. I would come home to the restaurant after school to have the customers helping me with my homework, enchanting me with their stories and sharing their own cultures through conversations over meals. It was the source of my passion for food as the most ubiquitous human experience.

With time, however, my passion for food waned. Upon graduating university, I believed that a career in human rights awaited me, but a serendipitous experience over a meal of Red Red Stew with a family in Ghana re-centered my life's path and brought me back home to food. Instead of pursuing a law degree, I set out to develop Kitchen Connection and focused my graduate studies on food.

After losing my wallet in Ghana, I was invited into the home of the Benneh family, where a beautiful, shared meal inspired a sense of nostalgia in me. As I maneuvered the last of the comforting Red Red Stew from the plate into my body, I thought of my childhood evenings spent sharing meals with strangers-turned-friends. I began to slow down and appreciate the meal even more: "Would I ever see the Benneh family again? Would I ever eat this delicious dish again?" I did not know what ingredients were in the recipe, but I knew that they played well together—so much so that they ignited a feeling of longing for a time that was not yet gone. I was overcome with the desire to re-create this meal and this experience again. I was determined to arrange a video chat with the Bennehs so that we could connect again over food and I could learn to prepare this dish with their guidance. *This,* I thought, *would be the closest thing to going back to Ghana and being there with them.* And then: *Why not give this gift to other people? To allow others to see the world, their world, using food as the means for connection and kinship?* Those questions gave rise to the birth of Kitchen Connection.

Today, Kitchen Connection unites people using food as the vehicle to greater discussions about the food system. We maintain that there cannot be a conversation about food without food on the table, so our online and in-person events bring people together to cook, share, unite and act in support of a better food system for all. Our goal is to meet people where they are: in libraries, schools, markets and in their own kitchens, using innovative approaches to alleviate some of the biggest challenges to our food system and recognizing the power that we all have to solve them.

There is a lot to learn from each other and from our experiences, much of which is embedded in our family histories. Oftentimes, the solution to some of our greatest concerns lies in our hearts and in the hearts (or experiences) of our neighbors—why not turn to them for inspiration? Issues that stem from a fractured food system affect all of us, so working collabo-ratively can help us create human-centered solutions at a global scale.

This book is an expression of that desire to look at each other with respect and gratitude. My hope is that the recipes in this cookbook bring the world home to you, and what the chefs, farmers, indigenous peoples and food justice advocates share in these pages is a window into the lives and cultures of the people behind the recipes. They have devoted their lives to improving the way we eat and how we think about food, forever. We hope that this can be an opportunity to harness that knowledge and to translate it into action.

Thank you for being a part of this journey with us.

Earlene Cruz
Founder and Executive Director, Kitchen Connection

Glossary of Terms

 VEGAN   VEGETARIAN   P PESCATARIAN

Biodiversity: Biological variety in all its forms, from the genetic makeup of plants and animals to cultural diversity. Biodiversity underpins all life on Earth.

Carbon footprint: The carbon footprint of a product is the quantity of greenhouse gases (GHG), expressed in carbon dioxide equivalent (CO_2e), emitted across the supply chain for a single unit of that product.

Climate change: A change of climate linked directly or indirectly to human activity that alters the composition of the global atmosphere and which is in addition to natural climate variability. In popular use, it is often used interchangeably with "global warming."

Deforestation: The long-term or permanent loss of forest cover caused and maintained by a human-induced or natural disturbance. Deforestation implies that the land is transformed for other uses, like agriculture, pasture and urban areas.

Double burden of malnutrition: The coexistence of undernutrition (nutrient deficiency) along with overweight, obesity or diet-related noncommunicable diseases within individuals, households and populations.

Food loss: The amount of food that is lost from its harvest, up to, but not including, the retail level, is referred to as food loss.

Food insecurity: A person is food insecure when they lack regular access to enough safe and nutritious food for normal growth and development and an active and healthy life. This may be due to unavailability of food and/or lack of resources to obtain food.

Food system: The food system includes all processes and infrastructure involved in feeding a population: growing, harvesting, processing, packaging, transporting, marketing, consumption and disposal of food and food-related items and its effects on the greater environment and society.

Food waste: The amount of food wasted at the consumer and retail level is referred to as food waste.

Global warming: The world's ongoing temperature rise as a result of society's emissions of greenhouse gases.

Green Revolution: An initiative that occurred between 1950 and the late 1960s, which increased agricultural production across the globe with a specific focus on crops that produce a high return.

Greenhouse gas (GHG): A gas that absorbs and emits radiant energy within the thermal infrared range. Greenhouse gases cause the greenhouse effect.

Healthy diet: Healthy diets are those diets that are of adequate quantity and quality to achieve optimal growth and development of all individuals and support functioning and physical, mental and social wellbeing at all life stages and physiological needs. Healthy diets are safe, diverse, balanced and based on nutritious foods.

*Healthy diets should include: at least 400g of fruit and vegetables per day (excluding starchy roots), legumes, nuts and whole grains. Energy intake needs to be balanced with expenditure (on average 2000-2500 kcal per person); less than 10 percent of total energy intake from free sugars; less than 5 grams of iodized salt per day; less than 30 percent of total energy intake from fats with intake from saturated fats representing less than 10 percent of total energy intake and trans-fats representing less than 1 percent of total energy intake.

*These recommendations should of course be tailored to fit a person's diet-related medical requirements.

Indigenous peoples: As expressed in the "FAO Policy on Indigenous and Tribal Peoples," indigenous peoples around the world are culturally distinct, yet they share a number of common values and a shared sense of purpose in their demand for internationally recognized rights and autonomy. These commonalities are expressed in the principles and rights, which have been articulated by indigenous representatives and are at the heart of the "UN Declaration on the Rights of Indigenous Peoples" (UNDRIP) as well as other international legal and standard-setting instruments. At the international level, there is overall understanding to refer to indigenous peoples based on certain characteristics that as per the UNDRIP (2007) could be summarized: Priority in time, with respect to occupation and use of a specific territory; the voluntary perpetuation of cultural distinctiveness, which may include aspects of language, social organization, religion and spiritual values, modes of production, laws and institutions; self-identification, as well as recognition by other groups, or by state authorities, as a distinct collectivity; and an experience of subjugation, marginalization, dispossession, exclusion or discrimination, whether or not these conditions persist.

Macronutrients: Macronutrients are nutrients that provide calories, or units of energy, and are required in large amounts to maintain body functions and carry out the activities of daily life. There are three broad classes of macronutrients: proteins, carbohydrates and fats.

Micronutrients: Micronutrients are vitamins and minerals needed by the body in very small amounts but critical to the function of the body. They perform a range of functions, including enabling the body to produce enzymes, hormones and other substances needed for normal growth and development. Deficiencies in iron, vitamin A and iodine are the most common around the world, particularly in children and pregnant women.

Supply chains: A system of organizations, people, activities and resources involved in supplying produce or food to a consumer.

Sustainable food system: A food system that delivers food security and nutrition for all in such a way that the economic, social and environmental bases to generate food security and nutrition for future generations are not compromised.

Sustainable healthy diets: Sustainable healthy diets are dietary patterns that promote all dimensions of individuals' health and wellbeing; have low levels of environmental pressure and impact; are accessible, safe and equitable; and are culturally acceptable.

Ultra-processed foods: Foods made up of snacks, drinks, ready meals and many other product types formulated mostly or entirely from substances extracted from foods or derived from food constituents.

I. The Food System

Resilient and Sustainable Food Systems

Food has the power to connect us, physically sustain us and emotionally nourish us. But when there is too little food or it does not meet our needs, the very essence of our lives is at stake. There is nothing that can make or break us—as individuals and communities—the way that food can.

Our driving question is: If there is enough food in the world to feed us all in a way that is both nutritious and good for the planet, why are so many still without consistently available, high-quality food?

The answer lies in the multilayered path that food takes on its way to our plates and the system that surrounds that process—what we call the *food system*.

Consider a banana. Where do its seeds come from? What happens to the seeds before they become fruit? Who decides that *this* kind of banana should make its way to our local market? Who then brings it to the market, and how? How far does it travel from the farm where it was cultivated to the market where it is sold, and then finally to the home where it reaches our tables?

Along this banana's journey, there are countless people and processes that craft its story. These important chapters are often overlooked and even unimaginable by the time the fruit finds its way to our plate. Among those unaccounted-for resources are land, seeds, water and air. Equally as instrumental is the labor of the grower, cultivator and transporter. With the rise of new technology, some people opt to have their foods delivered to them with the click of a button, without ever having to leave their homes and further disconnecting them from the source of the food and its story. Even after we eat a piece of fruit, we can ask ourselves: Is it necessary to throw away the peel? Must the seeds go in the trash? Are the stems truly undesirable?

All of these shifting pieces and their value-adding activities, from soil to producer to consumer, form the puzzle that we call the food system. If any of the pieces are missing or broken, the entire system is thrown off balance with harmful effects at the public, private, local and global levels.

What foods we consume, how much we consume and how much we lose and waste in the process have become critical considerations for people and planet.

Food insecurity doesn't just apply to those who do not have enough food. It also characterizes those who consume enough calories yet not enough nutrients. This paradox is growing quickly and is spurred on by a profit-driven, globalized food system. As we will explore further throughout the stories told in this cookbook, what we choose to eat has a tremendous impact on us—and also on the planet.

Food systems have understandably changed over time from our origins as hunter-gatherers to the development of stationary farmers to the modern industrialized system that we have at present. These systems will and should continue to morph and adapt to global lifestyle changes, but as they do, we should consider how we, as consumers, remain part of one whole and how our actions affect the entire system.

> The food system touches all of us, regardless of socioeconomic status, country of origin, gender, religion, political affiliation or cultural identity.

Let us consider the people:

- The farmer who cannot access a market because of a natural disaster or supply chain disruptions from a pandemic. Without a place to sell their crops, they might go hungry or be unable to feed their children or afford seeds for future production.
- The business owner or policymaker who wants to prioritize sustainable production but has to compromise due to conflicting agendas and funding priorities.
- The mother who lives near a supermarket overflowing with healthy leafy greens, fruits and legumes but is driven away by high prices and resorts to ultra-processed foods to feed her family.
- The country that once grew its own vegetables but due to climate change has to import things like tomatoes and greens, further contributing to the carbon burden and draining resources.
- The indigenous community whose government forces them to relocate after the discovery of valuable minerals in the region, stripping them of their sovereign land and foods like squashes, pulses and local game.
- The region that accepts donations of modified grains to feed its people during a famine, knowing that those grains provide insufficient nutrients and come with a new array of problems.
- The woman who is not allowed to own the farm that she would have inherited if she were male.
- The country that watches health costs associated with nutrition-related diseases like cancer, diabetes and heart disease rise with no end in sight and lacks the resources to afford care for all.
- The elderly person who fought in a war and is disabled, unable to work to afford three meals per day or a place to sleep.
- The family who has been displaced by conflict and is severed from their livelihood, community and history. As they migrate in search of food and hope, humanitarian agencies cannot reach them with aid.
- The siblings whose parents are not informed about the importance of fruits and vegetables that fall victim to unhealthy food marketing targeted at children. They carry unhealthy dietary patterns into adulthood, develop diseases and pass the same patterns on to their children.
- The smallholder farmer whose livelihood is squandered by the presence of a newly established industrial farm.

The list can continue with innumerable stories of *all of us* suffering from a broken food system.

WHAT ABOUT US?

Even amidst our own suffering, we cannot overlook the effects
of our food system on mountains, rivers, flora and fauna.
Let us consider the planet:

- The apples that require the emission of greenhouse gases for their transatlantic journey to market and leave a large carbon footprint that contributes to climate change.
- The eggs that are thrown away when restaurants close during a pandemic, while people in a nearby region do not have enough food to eat.
- The bees that are threatened by pesticides and climate change. When there are fewer bees to pollinate, we risk eliminating a critical process that allows us to enjoy important crops like almonds, apples, melons and broccoli.
- The population of fish that migrates or becomes endangered due to overfishing and climate change. What happens to the fish that once ate that fish—and the ones that ate those? What happens to the people who depended on them?
- The crops that no longer grow in their sovereign region because climate change has damaged the soil and made the growing conditions inhospitable. Without them, people go hungry and biodiversity is lost.
- The bird whose home forest is cut for the production of paper and is forced into the city in search of food, interacting with foods intended for human consumption and causing food contamination that makes the human population sick.
- The citrus fruits that are lost because of a lack of refrigeration or proper storage mechanisms. What about the water, sun and other natural resources that went into producing these wasted fruits?
- A bird species, like the passenger pigeon, that is hunted to endangerment or extinction by humans who benefit from advanced technology and treat them as trophies. What happens to the animals that relied on that bird for survival?
- The cows that are no longer cared for because they do not produce the best milk for human consumption.
- The landscape that transforms from a diverse region to an urban jungle because of a growing population that makes more money in cities. Who is to provide the local food for that large population? And what happens to the land that has been left behind or converted into concrete and steel skylines? What happens to the plants that used to live there, the ground animals and birds?
- The region that becomes increasingly polluted by vehicles and factories, resulting in chemical-laden food sources for local poultry. What happens to the humans who, in turn, eat those animals?
- The knowledge that, if food waste were a country in itself, it would be the third largest emitter of greenhouse gases in the world.

The list can continue with countless stories of the *planet* suffering from a broken food system.

WHAT ABOUT THE PLANET?

These scenarios demonstrate the intersectional relationships between things that grow and those who consume them and demands that these relationships return to a symbiotic agreement built upon mutual respect.

There will always be tradeoffs. It will never be perfect, but it can be better. And we can be a part of the solution. We can initiate positive change. You can be the change.

While global crises and profit motives have made food systems less resilient and equitable, it is not too late to be part of the solution. This requires multi-sectoral action with a unanimous goal to preserve our health and home. In other words, we need "all hands on deck."

Our first step is to make food systems more resilient. For instance, when there is a flood, there should be ways for the affected community to continue to eat and for local markets to continue to serve their population. Resilience also means that when the economy fluctuates, protections should be in place for those who are vulnerable. Those who have lost their jobs or—for any reason—are at risk of being food insecure should not go hungry.

Resilience requires that farmers have abundant structural support in the event they cannot access markets and that restaurants have a similar support system so that, under challenging situations, they are not forced to close their doors and abandon their employees. It means that animals and plants, whether we rely on them for food or not, should be cared for and respected. It means that we need to understand the factors contributing to climate change and act in ways that will alleviate it on individual and corporate levels. It means that access to safe and nutritious food should be a human right.

Seeing the gap that exists between true food system resilience and where we are now may feel daunting, but we can look at gaps as opportunities and remember that we don't need to fix it alone! Big businesses and governments have a large role to play, as policy initiatives and monetary redistribution will help narrow the gap. Federal programs like coordinated cash transfers, school feeding, access to healthcare, family-farming initiatives and incentives for farmers to move away from commodity dependence are proven structural solutions that should be adopted, and quickly.

As individuals, embracing simple, manageable habits—whether at the market or in the kitchen—can also make a significant impact. Instead of suggesting a "silver bullet," this book provides a rubric through which we can assess our relationship with food, for ourselves and our loved ones. We start with 75 recipes shared by a variety of food systems actors from around the world and designed to address these very issues and make it easier—and more delicious— to do our part as individuals. We also offer revolutionary climate calculations to demonstrate which foods are particularly carbon-friendly in the final chapter of the book and provide nutrition calculations and guidelines for all recipes in the index.

While not all of the ingredients for the recipes may be accessible to you, we encourage you to be creative and adapt them based on the ingredients that are, especially when you can source them locally, sustainably and in season.

There is no one-size-fits-all solution. Some communities would improve their health and that of the planet by eating less meat, while others could benefit from adding more of it to their diets. Some crops are wonderful for human health but require too much water in places where water is scarce. We are all part of a global balance, and solutions must be approached with that balance in mind.

Our goal as a society is to begin to intentionally question how our food choices impact our local and global food systems and our health. The answers lie in unadulterated nature, in the way that our ancestors ate and interacted with food as the sacred and nourishing vessel that it is. Re-evaluation starts with us—in our own kitchens and shopping baskets.

While we might not change the entire food system overnight, we can begin to move the needle in transformative ways. By talking to our local farmer or food purveyor about offering options that are more sustainable, we can drive demand. By encouraging curiosity, we can educate ourselves and one another. By cooking in new ways that are equally or more delicious and sharing that food, we can watch our health flourish. Together, we can. Together, we must.

INDIGENOUS PEOPLES: GUARDIANS OF BIODIVERSITY

More than 476 million people on the planet are considered indigenous. They live in more than 90 countries, and they belong to more than 5,000 different peoples. Each indigenous people has their own social structure and a unique way of perceiving life, which is called cosmogony. Do you know who the indigenous peoples in your country are?

Speaking more than 4000 different languages out of the 7000 spoken worldwide, indigenous peoples are incredibly diverse. Yet, there is one thing that the various indigenous peoples have in common: They hold a strong relation with Mother Earth.

For centuries, and in some cases even thousands of years, indigenous peoples have lived in very diverse ecosystems, including the savannah, rainforests, the Arctic tundra, deserts, mountains and plains. Currently, some of them also live in cities. Recent data estimates that indigenous peoples' territories hold 80 percent of the world's remaining biodiversity. How incredible is this?

Food diversity is strongly related to flora and fauna diversity. Therefore, indigenous peoples hold unique food systems that are rooted in their territories' biodiversity. Indigenous peoples are hunters, farmers, gatherers, fishers, herders and pastoralists, among others. They utilize different techniques to generate food for their communities while preserving the natural resources in their territories, as it is the foundation of their food systems.

You can see why indigenous peoples are known as guardians of Mother Earth, but there is more.

The land where they belong shapes their indigenous identity, culture and traditions. They rely on local resources, specifically plants, for medicinal use and to support their livelihoods. Their peoples' stories are related to the ancestral land they inhabit, to the seas, the lakes and the lagoons surrounding them and to the animals and spirits with whom they share the territory. Their ceremonies and handicrafts also tell a story of their territory, their cosmogony and their relationship with Mother Earth.

Indigenous peoples' unique food systems include the appropriate management of their ancestral land, their traditional knowledge—which is passed from one generation to another—their cosmogony and their livelihoods.

There is wisdom to glean from indigenous peoples that we can embrace and carry forward to protect the health of the Earth.

In order to support indigenous peoples, the first step is to acknowledge them and to respect their unique connection to the lands that they inhabit.

When you read the different indigenous peoples' recipes and stories in this book, imagine the wonderful ecosystem they inhabit, the amazing biodiversity that is in their territories and the strong relationship they have with Mother Earth.

SAFFRON CHICKEN WITH FREEKEH

Zahra Abdalla
Iran and Sudan

Yield: 6 servings
Active time: 1 hour
Total time: 2 hours

Multinational author and food blogger Zahra Abdalla hosts food-related media pro-grams from her base in Dubai, UAE. Inspired by the Arabic and Iranian cuisines from her childhood, Abdalla creates beautiful, updated classics like this one-pot dish that artfully fuses the two cultures and reduces waste. The chicken is spiced with a heady mix of cinnamon, turmeric and Arabic 7-spice powder—a blend that is also called baharat or bokharat, which can be found at Middle Eastern grocers or online. It is paired with nutty, nutritious freekeh, an ancient grain that Abdalla says promotes digestive and planetary health.

Wash the freekeh well in a bowl of cold water and drain in a fine-mesh sieve. Repeat. Return to the bowl, add enough water to cover by 1 inch (2.5 cm) and let stand for about 1 hour. Drain well and set aside.

In a small bowl, whisk together the 7-spice powder, ground cinna-mon, turmeric, 1½ teaspoons salt, and ½ teaspoon pepper. Sprinkle the spice mixture all over the chicken and set aside.

In a 5- to 6-quart (4.8 to 5.7 liter) Dutch oven or flameproof casserole, preferably enameled cast iron, heat the olive oil over medium heat. Add the onions, cinnamon stick and cardamom pods and cook, stirring occa-sionally, until the onions are soft but not browned, about 3 minutes. Stir in the ginger and garlic. Add the freekeh and stir well. Cook, stirring oc-casionally, until the freekeh is sticking lightly to the pot, about 3 minutes. Combine the chicken stock, rose water, saffron and ½ teaspoon salt. Pour over the freekeh and stir well, especially at the bottom of the pot.

Nestle the chicken pieces in the freekeh mixture. (It can be closely packed as the chicken will shrink during cooking.) Bring to a boil. Cover tightly and reduce the heat to medium-low. Simmer on low without stir-ring until the freekeh has absorbed most of the liquid and the chicken is fully cooked (it will show just a little pink when pierced at the bone with a small sharp knife), 40 to 45 minutes. Remove the cover during the last 5 minutes to cook off any excess liquid—the freekeh should be moist but not soupy. Remove from the heat, cover tightly again and let stand for 5 minutes. Discard the cinnamon stick. Sprinkle with the cashews, al-monds, figs, apricots, golden raisins and parsley. Serve hot.

2 cups (322 g) whole freekeh

1 teaspoon Arabic 7-spice powder

1 teaspoon ground cinnamon

1 teaspoon ground turmeric

Salt and freshly ground black pepper

4 sustainably sourced bone-in chicken drumsticks (about 1 ½ pounds / 675 g total), skin removed

4 sustainably sourced bone-in chicken thighs (about 2 pounds / 900 g total), skin removed

2 tablespoons olive oil

2 medium yellow onions, diced

1 cinnamon stick

2 cardamom pods

1 (½-inch / 1.25 cm) piece ginger, peeled and grated

2 garlic cloves, minced

2½ cups (600 ml) chicken stock

1 teaspoon rose water

¼ teaspoon crushed saffron

¼ cup (30 g) toasted cashews

¼ cup (35 g) toasted almonds

3 dried figs, roughly chopped

3 dried apricots, roughly chopped

2 tablespoons golden raisins

Fresh flat-leaf parsley leaves, roughly chopped

CEDAR-PLANKED ARCTIC CHAR WITH GRILLED VEGETABLES

Sheila Flaherty
Inuit Community
Canada

Yield: 6 servings
Active time: 1 hour
Total time: 1 hour, plus 1 hour soaking time

For the pistachio-parsley topping:

1 cup (128 g) salted pistachios

4 shallots, roughly chopped

1 ½ cups (125 g) chopped fresh flat-leaf parsley leaves

½ cup (25 g) chopped fresh dill, plus more for serving

1 tablespoon freshly grated lemon zest

2 tablespoons fresh lemon juice

1 tablespoon olive oil

½ teaspoon sea salt

For the grilled vegetables:

2 small zucchini, roughly chopped

6 cremini mushrooms, roughly chopped

1 red bell pepper, roughly chopped

1 small red onion, roughly chopped

2 cups (275 g) grape tomatoes

8 garlic cloves, peeled

¼ cup (60 ml) olive oil

Sea salt and freshly ground black pepper

For the cedar planked arctic char:

6 (4-ounce / 112 g) pieces sustainably sourced boneless skin-on arctic char

Sea salt and freshly ground black pepper

Coarse sea salt to prevent sticking

2 cedar planks

Sheila Flaherty is an Inuit harvester, hunter and chef in Iqaluit, Nunavut, Canada, also known as "the place of many Arctic char." She is a Director at Indigenous Culinary of Associated Nations, an organization that harnesses the power of digital media and the sharing of cultural experiences to promote indigenous culinary experiences. With many Inuit households resorting to supermarket foods for their low cost and convenience, Sheila is dedicated to growing a network of harvesters and hunters that can create a self-sustaining, traditional economy. Wild arctic char is rich in omega-3 fatty acids and is fished year-round by Inuit communities. If you are unable to source sustainable arctic char in your area, salmon or steelhead trout are good alternatives.

About 1 hour before cooking, soak the cedar planks in water.

Make the pistachio-parsley topping:

In a food processor, pulse the pistachios and shallots until minced, about 30 seconds. Add the parsley, dill, lemon zest and juice, olive oil and salt. Pulse again until the parsley and dill are minced, about 1 minute. Transfer to a bowl and set aside.

Grill the vegetables:

Preheat the grill to medium-high, about 375°F (190°C).

In a large bowl, combine the zucchini, mushrooms, bell pepper, red onion, grape tomatoes and garlic. Drizzle with the olive oil, season with salt and pepper and toss to coat. Spread the vegetables on a sheet pan that will fit on your grill. Set the sheet pan directly on the grill rack and grill, covered, until the vegetables develop a good char, about 10 minutes. Remove from the grill and keep warm. Leave the grill set to medium-high, about 375°F (190°C).

Grill the arctic char:

Make sure all the pin bones are removed from the fish. Wipe the skin sides dry with a paper towel, then season generously with salt and pepper.

Set the cedar planks directly on the grill rack and let heat until they start to crackle, 3 to 4 minutes. Flip the planks over and sprinkle some coarse sea salt on each one to prevent the fish from sticking. Arrange the fish pieces on the salted planks. Spread the pistachio-parsley topping evenly on top of the fish and grill, covered, until the sides of the fish feel firm to the touch, 12 to 15 minutes. Serve immediately sprinkled with dill and with the warm grilled vegetables on the side.

RED KIDNEY BEANS AND RICE CURRY

Mbali Nwoko
South Africa

Yield: 4 servings
Active time: 30 minutes
Total time: 45 Minutes

Mbali Nwoko is a South African farmer and writer from Johannesburg who is passionate about food security. Her recipes utilize plant-based ingredients that promote crop rotation and good soil health. She also founded Green Terrace, an agribusiness dedicated to providing high-quality vegetable crops to retailers and produce markets across South Africa. Nwoko's recipe is a comforting classic that she hopes will quickly become a staple on your table too.

In a medium saucepan, combine the rice, red kidney beans, chicken broth, half the garlic and the butter and bring to a boil. Cover, reduce the heat to low and simmer until the rice is tender, 10 to 15 minutes. Remove from the heat and let stand.

Meanwhile, in a large, deep frying pan, heat the canola oil over medium-high heat. Add the onion, celery and the rest of the garlic and cook, stirring, until soft but not browned, about 6 minutes. Add the cumin and paprika, season with salt and pepper and cook, stirring, until fragrant, about 1 minute. Add the tomatoes and coconut cream and bring to a simmer. Add the broccoli, cover and cook, stirring occasionally, until tender, about 8 minutes. Add the rice and bean mixture and stir to combine. Season with salt and pepper and serve.

1 cup (180 g) long grain white rice

1 (14-ounce / 400 g) can red kidney beans, drained

2 cups (480 ml) chicken broth

2 garlic cloves, chopped

1 teaspoon unsalted butter

2 tablespoons canola oil

½ white or yellow onion, chopped

2 celery stalks, chopped

1 tablespoon ground cumin

1 tablespoon smoked paprika

Salt and freshly ground black pepper

4 medium tomatoes, diced

2 tablespoons coconut cream

1 head broccoli, cut into small florets

THE ZIMMERN FAMILY MATZO BALL SOUP

Andrew Zimmern
United States

Yield: 8 servings
Active time: 1 hour
Total time: 3 hours and 45 minutes

For the chicken soup:

12 cups (2.8 liters) chicken broth, preferably homemade

1 (3 pound / 1.3 kg) sustainably sourced chicken

For the matzo balls:

1 ¼ cups (160 g) matzo meal

½ teaspoon granulated garlic

½ teaspoon baking powder

½ teaspoon baking soda

Kosher salt

¼ cup (60 ml) schmaltz (melted chicken fat) or vegetable oil

¼ cup (50 g) grated yellow onion (about 1 small onion)

5 sustainably sourced large eggs, 3 separated

1 tablespoon vegetable oil, for forming the matzo balls

To serve:

4 large dill sprigs, plus chopped dill for serving

4 large flat-leaf parsley sprigs, plus chopped parsley for serving

3 large carrots, thinly sliced

3 large celery ribs, thinly sliced

2 yellow onions, diced

1 medium rutabaga, peeled and diced

Kosher salt and freshly ground black pepper

Andrew Zimmern is a chef, writer, TV personality and food educator from the United States, who has devoted his life to exploring and promoting cultural acceptance, tolerance and understanding through food. He calls this family recipe, inspired by his grandmother and lovingly tweaked for decades, one of his five favorite foods. While matzo ball soup is traditionally served at Passover, Zimmern calls it a year-round treasure and notes that its healing powers have earned it the name "Jewish penicillin." His trick for making floaters not sinkers—his preference when it comes to matzo balls—is to add air by gently folding in beaten egg whites.

Make the chicken soup:

In a large stockpot, bring the chicken broth to a simmer. Add the chicken, breast side up, and return the broth to a simmer. Cover the pot and adjust the heat as needed to maintain a very low simmer. Continue gently simmering until the chicken is cooked through, about 1 hour and 20 minutes. Carefully transfer the hot chicken to a bowl, cover loosely and let cool.

Remove the broth from the heat and let cool for 20 minutes. Strain through a fine-mesh strainer into a heatproof bowl, then return it to the pot. Skim off any fat, as needed.

Pull the meat off the cooled chicken, shred it into bite-size pieces and set aside; discard the chicken carcass.

Meanwhile, make the matzo balls:

In a large bowl, stir together the matzo meal, granulated garlic, baking powder, baking soda and 2 teaspoons salt.

In a medium bowl, whisk the schmaltz and onion with the 2 whole eggs and the 3 egg yolks.

In a separate bowl, beat the 3 egg whites and a pinch of salt with an electric mixer until stiff peaks form.

Stir the schmaltz mixture into the matzo mixture, then stir in one-third of the beaten egg whites until incorporated. Gently fold in the remaining whites until no streaks remain. Press a sheet of plastic wrap directly onto the surface of the batter and refrigerate until firm, at least 40 minutes or overnight.

In a small bowl, combine the 1 tablespoon of vegetable oil with 1 tablespoon of water.

Line a sheet pan with plastic wrap. Scoop tablespoon-sized mounds of the matzo batter onto the baking sheet. Using the oil-and-water mixture to keep your hands moist, roll each scoop of batter into a ball, handling them as gently as possible. Refrigerate while you cook the vegetables.

Finish the soup:

Return the chicken broth to a simmer. Tie the dill and parsley sprigs together with kitchen string then add to the pot, along with the carrot, celery, onion and rutabaga. Season generously with salt and pepper and bring to a boil. Reduce the heat to medium-low, cover and simmer for 10 minutes. Add the matzo balls, gently stir and return to a simmer, adjusting the heat as needed. Continue simmering, turning the matzo balls a few times, until they are plump and cooked through, 20 to 25 minutes. Remove and discard the parsley and dill sprigs and gently add the shredded chicken. Season with salt and pepper and serve sprinkled with chopped parsley and dill.

MORINGA PESTO PASTA

Zoe Adjonyoh
Ghana

Yield: 4 servings (plus extra pesto)
Active time: 40 minutes
Total time: 1 hour

Zoe Adjonyoh is a chef, writer and food justice activist dedicated to rebuilding a more equitable food system. With her exquisite recipes, she breaks the boundaries of what "African Food" is expected to be and works to correct the cultural representation of Africa's superfoods, while supporting and promoting black-owned businesses and African farmers.

In her work, Adjonyoh brings the backstory of the food and the food producer to life. By connecting the farmer to the consumer, she provides the consumer with the resources needed to incorporate exciting and novel ingredients into healthful every-day meals. With this recipe, Adjonyoh supports sustainable agriculture by bringing together a variety of African seeds, spices and vegetables to create a nutritious and flavorful meal.

Preheat the oven to 350°F (180°C).

On a sheet pan, toss the cashews with 1 teaspoon of the olive oil and the suya spice and bake until golden, about 18 minutes. Let cool completely.

In a food processor, pulse the cooled cashews until crushed. Gradually add the garlic, Scotch bonnet chilis, arugula, lemon zest and juice, moringa powder and ½ cup (120 ml) of the olive oil, pausing to scrape down the bowl as needed. Blend until a chunky paste forms. While pulsing, gradually add the remaining ¼ cup (60 ml) of olive oil, pulsing until the oil is fully incorporated but the pesto is still a bit chunky. Season with the salt and alligator pepper.

Bring a large pot of salted water to a boil. Add the pasta and cook, according to the package directions, until al dente, about 8 minutes. Drain the pasta, reserving about ¼ cup (60 ml) of the pasta water, then toss while still hot with about 2 cups (480 g) of the pesto. Add some of the reserved pasta water as needed to combine. Sprinkle with fresh basil and serve.

Refrigerate extra pesto in an airtight container, covered with a thin layer of olive oil, for up to 3 days, or freeze for up to 1 month.

SUYA SPICE

Yield: Makes 1 ⅔ cups (200 g)

In a small bowl, whisk together the ground cashews, cayenne, smoked paprika, ginger, garlic powder, onion powder, nutmeg, cloves, alligator pepper, and salt.

Store in an airtight container in a cool dark place for up to 6 months. Use on meats and veggies for grilling or roasting.

For the pasta:

2 ½ cups (300 g) cashews

¾ cup plus 1 teaspoon (185 ml) extra-virgin olive oil

2 tablespoons Suya Spice (recipe follows)

2 garlic cloves, peeled and smashed

1 to 2 Scotch bonnet or habanero chilis, deseeded and roughly chopped

5 ounces (140 g) baby arugula

½ teaspoon freshly grated lemon zest

3 tablespoons fresh lemon juice

2 teaspoons moringa powder

1 ½ teaspoons sea salt

1 ½ teaspoons freshly ground alligator pepper (grains of paradise)

1 pound (450 g) dried pasta, such as rigatoni or penne

Fresh basil leaves, for serving

For the Suya Spice:

¾ cup (90 g) toasted cashews, finely ground

2 tablespoons ground cayenne pepper

¼ cup (24 g) smoked paprika

¼ cup (24 g) ground ginger

2 tablespoons garlic powder

2 tablespoons onion powder

1 teaspoon ground nutmeg

½ teaspoon ground cloves

1 teaspoon freshly ground alligator pepper (grains of paradise)

1 teaspoon fine sea salt

SOUPE PAYSANNE
Soup Jaden—Red Cabbage, Yam, Green Peas and Spinach Soup

Natacha Gomez
Haiti

Yield: 4 to 6 servings
Active time: 45 minutes
Total time: 1 hour

3 sprigs fresh flat-leaf parsley

3 sprigs fresh thyme

1 fresh or dried bay leaf

1 tablespoon onion powder

1 teaspoon garlic powder

1 teaspoon ground cloves

¼ red cabbage, roughly chopped

4 cups (960 ml) vegetable broth

1 tablespoon fresh lime juice

Salt and freshly ground pepper

1 yam or sweet potato, peeled and cubed

1 green (unripe) plantain (about 7 ounces / 200 g), peeled and cubed

2 ears corn, each cut into 4 pieces

3 tablespoons vegetable oil, plus more for brushing

1 bunch spinach, stems and any thick veins removed and leaves roughly chopped

1 leek, finely chopped and well washed

1 shallot, finely diced

½ teaspoon Scotch bonnet paste or a few drops of hot sauce

1 cup (128 g) all-purpose flour

1 tablespoon brown sugar

2 medium carrots, peeled and diced

1 cup (145 g) fresh or frozen green peas

For tips to peel the plantains, see note on page 48.

Natacha Gomez is a Haitian chef and climate action activist who develops traditional, authentic dishes with a nutritious twist. Haiti struggles with many of the consequences of climate change and environmental degradation, such as increased occurrences of severe hurricanes, that impact crop production and economic health. With this recipe, Gomez helps support the local economy and community health. Called Bouyon Jaden in French Creole, Soupe Paysanne in French, and Soup Jaden in English, it incorporates seasonal and widely available ingredients that are an ode to the hard work of farmers, who care for their communities and families by producing nutritious foods.

Use kitchen string to tie the parsley, thyme and bay leaf together in a small bundle.

In a large, heavy pot, combine the herb bundle with the onion powder, garlic powder, cloves, cabbage and vegetable broth. Bring to a boil and then lower the heat and simmer until the cabbage is tender, about 8 minutes. Remove and discard the herb bundle. Strain the cabbage, reserving the broth, and set aside. Add the lime juice to the cabbage broth, season with salt and pepper, and keep warm.

Fill a medium saucepan with 3 cups (720 ml) of water and bring to a boil over high heat. Add the yam, green plantain and corn then reduce the heat and simmer until tender, about 8 minutes. Transfer the yam to a medium bowl and set aside. Transfer the green plantain and corn to a large bowl and set aside. Reserve the yam broth.

Brush a sheet pan with oil.

In a large skillet, heat 2 tablespoons of the vegetable oil over medium-high heat until shimmering. Add the cooked cabbage, along with the spinach, leek, shallot and Scotch bonnet paste and cook, stirring, until the vegetables are tender, 5 to 6 minutes. Season with salt and pepper. Transfer to a large bowl. Add the flour and ¼ cup (60 ml) of the reserved yam broth. Stir to combine and then knead with your hands until a firm ball of dough forms. Using wet hands, shape the dough into roughly golf ball–sized round dumplings— you should get about 15 dumplings—and place on the prepared sheet pan.

Place any remaining yam broth in a small saucepan and bring to a boil over high heat. Working in batches, add the dumplings and cook until firm, about 5 minutes. Remove from the yam broth and keep warm.

In a medium skillet, heat the remaining 1 tablespoon of vegetable oil and the brown sugar. Add the cooked yam, along with the carrots and peas, and cook, stirring, until the yam is lightly golden, 3 to 4 minutes. Season with salt and pepper. Remove from the heat and keep warm.

Divide the yam, carrots, peas, green plantains, corn and dumplings among 4 to 6 bowls. Pour some hot cabbage broth into each bowl and serve hot.

TALKAN

Yana Tannagasheva
Shor Community
South-West Serbia, Russia

Yield: About 34 balls
Active time: 30 minutes
Total time: 45 minutes plus 1 ½ hours chilling

Yana Tannagasheva is a representative of the Shor Indigenous People of Southern Siberia who works to preserve the traditional recipes of her community. In her native lands, open-pit coal mining is destroying the water quality and food supply, so the local population must cook and eat whatever products are available to them. From the root word "talka," meaning "to grind," this talkan recipe combines ground barley with butter, honey and pine nuts to create a completely unique morsel that is enjoyed at any time of day by the Shor people.

3 cups (400 g) barley flour

Salt

1 stick plus 6 tablespoons (196 g) unsalted butter, melted

⅔ cup (150 ml) honey

¾ cup (100 g) pine nuts

In a medium saucepan, combine the barley flour and ½ teaspoon salt and toast over medium heat, stirring constantly, until the flour smells toasted, 4 to 5 minutes. Remove from the heat.

In a small saucepan, combine the melted butter and honey over low heat and cook, stirring constantly, until warm, about 3 minutes. Pour over the barley, then add the pine nuts and stir to fully combine. Season with ¼ to ½ teaspoon salt. Transfer the dough to a bowl, cover and refrigerate for 15 minutes.

To shape the talkan, scoop a small amount into one hand and squeeze, as if squeezing a walnut in your palm, to create a roughly 1-inch (2.5 cm) ball. Arrange on a sheet pan and repeat until all the dough is shaped into balls. Refrigerate until solid and chilled, 1 to 1 ½ hours. Serve chilled.

APPLE CRANBERRY PECAN WILD RICE PILAF

Mariah Gladstone
Blackfeet Nation Community
United States

Yield: 4 to 6 servings
Active time: 10 minutes
Total time: 50 minutes

1 cup (150 g) hand-harvested wild rice

½ cup (80 g) dried cranberries

2 cups (480 ml) vegetable broth

2 cups (480 ml) apple juice

¼ teaspoon dried thyme

¼ teaspoon dried oregano

2 tablespoons sunflower oil

1/4 teaspoon freshly ground black pepper

1 granny smith apple, peeled, cored and diced

½ cup (56 g) pecans, chopped

3 garlic cloves, minced

Salt and freshly ground black pepper

Mariah Gladstone produces "Indigination," an online cooking show that highlights traditional indigenous foods and encourages food sovereignty. As a member of the Blackfeet Nation, she draws attention to the many health consequences indigenous communities face as a result of disruptions to their native food systems and advocates for re-indigenizing our plates from the ground up. For this fall-flavored side dish, Gladstone uses wild rice that is hand-harvested by indigenous people in the Great Lakes region. Combined with tart, crunchy apples and sweet cranberries, this nutty rice is a harvest season delight.

In a medium pot, combine the wild rice, dried cranberries, broth, apple juice, thyme, oregano, 1 tablespoon of the sunflower oil and ¼ teaspoon pepper and bring to a rapid simmer. Cover and continue simmering until the liquid is completely absorbed, about 40 minutes. If the rice is done after 40 minutes but there is still liquid left in the pot, uncover, raise the heat, and quickly cook off any remaining liquid.

Meanwhile, in a small frying pan, heat the remaining 1 tablespoon sunflower oil over medium heat. Add the apples, pecans and garlic and cook until the apples are soft, about 5 minutes. Add to the cooked rice, stirring to combine. Season generously with salt and pepper and serve warm.

PEPPER-BRAISED FISH

Dũng Võ Ngọc and Thanh Vuong
Vietnam

Yield: 4 to 6 servings
Active time: 30 minutes
Cook time: 45 to 55 minutes

Dũng Võ Ngọc and Thanh Vuong are young spice farmers in Krông Năng, Đăk Lăk province, Vietnam. They use organic growing practices like intercropping with coffee and chili pepper plants, grazing chickens and ducks and nitrogen-fixing trees to support their pepper vines and in an effort to combat pesticide contamination of the food supply that is common in Vietnam. This recipe combines snakehead fish, a species native to Vietnam, and a warm, fiery pepper that they grow on their farm, but you can use any sustainably sourced firm fish to make this dish your own.

In a bowl, combine 1 tablespoon of the fish sauce, 1 tablespoon of the sugar, 1 tablespoon of the vegetable oil, the ginger, the white parts of the scallions, 1 teaspoon salt and 1 teaspoon ground pepper. Add the fish, stir to coat in the marinade, cover and refrigerate for at least 30 minutes but preferably 1 to 2 hours.

Meanwhile, soak the dried shiitake mushrooms in hot water until soft, about 30 minutes. Remove the mushrooms and chop if large (you can strain the soaking liquid and reserve it for another use). Set aside.

In a small pot, combine the remaining 1 ½ teaspoons of sugar with 2 tablespoon of water over medium-high heat and cook, stirring to dissolve the sugar, until the sugar turns dark brown, about 2 minutes. Add the whole black peppercorns, 1 teaspoon ground pepper, and the remaining 1 teaspoon of fish sauce. Stir until the sugar is completely dissolved.

In another large pot, heat the remaining 2 tablespoons of vegetable oil over medium-high heat. Add the galangal and spread it out to create a layer on the bottom of the pot. Add the mushrooms, spreading them out to create a second layer. Arrange the fish on top of the mushrooms. Add the chilis and then pour the sugar mixture, along with ⅔ cup (150 ml) of water, over the fish. Raise the heat to medium-high and bring to a simmer. Lower the heat and continue simmering until most of the liquid cooks off, 30 to 35 minutes. Sprinkle with the scallion greens and serve hot with rice.

1 tablespoon plus 1 teaspoon fish sauce

1 tablespoon plus 1 ½ teaspoons sugar

3 tablespoons vegetable oil

1 (2-inch / 5 cm) piece ginger, thinly sliced

6 scallions, white and green parts separated and roughly chopped

Salt and freshly ground black pepper

4 to 6 (6-ounce / 170 g) sustainably sourced, skinless firm fish fillets, such as salmon, catfish, bluefish or mackerel

1 ounce (28 g) dried shiitake mushrooms (approximately 12 mushrooms)

½ teaspoon whole black peppercorns

1 (1-inch / 2.5 cm) piece galangal, thinly sliced (peeled if the skin is particularly thick)

1 to 2 fresh red chilis, thinly sliced, or more to taste

Cooked jasmine rice, for serving

SALATAT BAZINJAN
Aubergine Salad

Omer Eltigani
Nubian Community
Sudan

Yield: 4 servings
Active time: 20 minutes
Total time: 20 minutes, plus 30 minutes to 1 hour draining time

2 large aubergine (eggplants; about 2 ¼ pounds / 1 kg total), peeled and cut into ¾-inch (2 cm) cubes

Salt and freshly ground black pepper

Canola oil, as needed, for deep-frying

2 tablespoons smooth peanut butter

2 tablespoons fresh lime juice, plus more as needed

1 garlic clove, minced

¼ teaspoon ground cumin, plus more as needed

1 tablespoon full or low-fat Greek yogurt, plus more as needed

1 scallion, finely chopped, for serving

Chopped peanuts, for serving (optional)

Pita bread or other flatbread, for serving

Omer Eltigani is a Nubian home cook who works to increase the global exposure of the cuisine and culture of Sudan. As an advocate for soil health, Eltigani notes that the ingredients in this salad can be grown organically in most climates. The aubergine in this recipe fuses with lime, garlic and local dakwa, or peanut butter, for an indulgent and unique dish that blends Arab and Turkish culinary practices. It is best as a side dish or served as a dip, alongside other dishes.

Line a sheet pan with paper towels.

Spread the eggplant on a clean work surface, and then toss with a generous sprinkling of salt. Spread on the prepared sheet pan and cover with paper towels. Place a second sheet pan on top, weigh it down with a few heavy plates or cans, and let the eggplant drain for 30 minutes to 1 hour. Pat the eggplant dry with fresh towels.

Fill a large pot with enough canola oil to come at least 2 inches (5 cm) up the sides. Place over medium-high heat and bring to 350°F (180°C) on a deep-fry thermometer. Line a clean sheet pan with a double layer of paper towels and place it near the stove.

Working in batches, carefully add the eggplant cubes to the hot oil and deep-fry over high heat, turning occasionally, until golden brown all over and tender, 3 to 4 minutes. Using a slotted spoon, transfer the eggplant to the paper towel–lined sheet pan to drain and cool. Continue to fry the eggplant, adjusting the heat as needed to keep the oil at 350°F (180°C).

In a small bowl, combine the peanut butter and 6 tablespoons (90 ml) warm water and let stand for 2 minutes, then whisk to loosen the peanut butter. Add the lime juice, garlic, cumin and yogurt, and whisk to combine. (Alternatively, combine the ingredients in a blender.)

Transfer the fried eggplant to a large serving bowl. Add the dressing and use a large, slotted spoon to coarsely mash the eggplant and mix in the dressing. Season with salt and pepper and add more lime juice, cumin or yogurt, as needed to balance the salad. Sprinkle with the scallions and peanuts, if desired, and serve with pita or other flatbread.

KUNA FISH AND VEGETABLE STEW

Aleida Robles
Kuna Community
Panama

Yield: 6 servings
Active time: 45 minutes
Total time: 1 hour and 15 minutes

As an indigenous home cook, Aleida Robles seeks to share the traditions of the Kuna people living in Panama. Traditionally, the Kuna people, a community of about 300,000, rely on locally harvested, sustainable fish and produce as their main sources of food and income, but climate change poses an increasing threat to their lifestyle. Robles hopes that by working together, we can improve the ecosystems that support our food system. Her recipe for grilled fish served with a tropical stew utilizes locally sourced ingredients that are native to Panama, including bananas, coconut and red snapper. It is a fun feast and fuels our diet with healthful nutrients, such as potassium, vitamin C and B vitamins. In Panama, Robles would use culantro, but she suggests the more widely available cilantro (coriander) as a good substitute.

3 white young coconuts

3 green (unripe) bananas, peeled and cut into 1-inch (2.5 cm) slices

18 ounces (500 g) fresh or frozen yuca (cassava root), peeled and cut into chunks

1 (13.5 fluid ounce / 398 ml) can coconut milk

2 limes

2 to 3 tablespoons hot sauce, plus more for serving

Salt and freshly ground black pepper

6 (5-ounce) sustainably sourced skin-on red snapper fillets or other firm white fish, such as haddock, pollock, black cod or striped bass

Vegetable oil

Chopped fresh cilantro (coriander) leaves, for serving

One at a time, hold each young coconut on its side on a cutting board with the pointed top facing toward your dominant hand.

Holding the bottom of the coconut, and using a cleaver or a sturdy chef's knife with your dominant hand, strike the coconut repeatedly, turning it to create a seam of cuts about 1 inch (2.5 cm) below the pointed top.

Chip pieces off to expose a circle of white flesh. Cut or pierce a hole in the flesh and pour the coconut water into a large bowl. Strain the coconut water to remove any coconut fragments and set aside. Using a spoon, scrape all of the white coconut meat away from the shell. Cut the coconut meat into bite-size chunks. Discard the husk and repeat with the remaining coconuts. (Alternatively, set a cleaver on top of the coconut in line with the hole and hit the cleaver with a rubber mallet to split the shell. Set tools aside and pry the two sides apart with your hands to access the coconut flesh more easily.)

In a large pot, combine the coconut chunks, green banana and yuca. Add the strained coconut water and the coconut milk and bring to a boil. Reduce the heat to medium and cook until the yuca is starting to fall apart, about 30 minutes. Squeeze 1 lime over the stew, then season with hot sauce, salt and pepper. Keep warm.

Meanwhile, preheat a grill to medium-high (400 to 450°F / 200 to 230°C). Generously brush both sides of the fish fillets with vegetable oil and season generously with salt and pepper.

Oil the grill rack. Place the fish, skin side down, on the grill and cook, flipping once, until it easily flakes with a fork, 3 to 5 minutes per side.

Cut the remaining lime in half and cut one half into wedges. Squeeze the other half over the fish, season with salt and pepper, and sprinkle with cilantro. Serve with the lime wedges, coconut stew and hot sauce.

SPIRULINA-TOSSED VEGETABLE SALAD

Alma Roblin
France

Yield: 4 to 6 servings
Active time: 20 minutes
Total time: 20 minutes

- 2 sweet potatoes, cut into ½-inch-thick (1.25 cm) rounds
- Salt and freshly ground white pepper
- ½ red onion, thinly sliced
- ¾ pound (340 g) white button mushrooms, thinly sliced
- 1 (14-ounce / 400 g) can chickpeas, drained
- 1 medium zucchini, cut into small cubes
- 1 cup (240 ml) fresh lime juice (from about 10 limes)
- 4 garlic cloves, minced
- 1 (2-inch / 5 cm) piece ginger, peeled and grated
- 1 red limo or habanero chili, finely sliced
- 2 tablespoons chopped fresh cilantro (coriander) leaves, plus more for serving
- 1 tablespoon spirulina, dissolved in 3 tablespoons cold water

Alma Roblin is a French farmer and entrepreneur living in Perú, where she grows high-quality, traceable spirulina and cushuro. Roblin shares her environment-friendly harvesting and water recycling methods with other farmers in her region. The unique geography of Perú allows an abundance of nutrient-rich foods to be produced across its different regions, including tarwi, an Andean legume that Roblin would typically use to make this vegan dish. She suggests chickpeas as a more widely available substitute. Pouring hot water over the vegetables cooks them ever so slightly and gives them a smooth texture. To maximize the flavor of this dish, Roblin recommends reserving and using any liquid released from the ginger as you peel and grate it.

Bring a medium saucepan of water to a boil. Add the sweet potatoes, reduce the heat, and simmer until tender, 10 to 12 minutes. Drain the potatoes, season with salt and white pepper, and set aside to cool.

In a small bowl, combine the red onion with enough cold water to cover and let stand for 10 minutes to mellow the onion's harshness.

Bring 2 cups (480 ml) of water to a boil in a small saucepan. In a large colander set in the sink, combine the mushrooms, chickpeas and zucchini. Pour the boiling water over them. Let drain, then transfer to a large bowl.

In a small bowl, whisk together the lime juice, garlic, ginger, limo chili, cilantro and the dissolved spirulina. Add to the mushroom mixture. Drain the red onion and add to the mushroom mixture. Toss to combine and then let stand for 10 minutes. Season with salt and white pepper. Sprinkle with cilantro and serve with the cooled sweet potatoes on the side.

ENKUM

Rachael Sintamei Yiaile
Maasai Community
Kenya

Yield: 4 servings
Active time: 25 minutes
Total time: 1 hour

Rachael Sintamei Yiaile is a home cook from the Maasai indigenous community in Kenya. Frequent droughts and social unrest make food expensive in her hometown, so she strives to share recipes that are cost-effective and health-supportive. In this recipe, pumpkin leaves—which provide vitamins A and C—are mashed with corn, green beans, potatoes and savory sautéed scallions to create a vibrant starchy side dish. Enkum is best served with steamed cabbage or a protein-rich stew.

Fill a medium saucepan with water and bring to a boil over high heat. Add the corn and green beans and boil until soft, about 15 minutes. Transfer the corn and green beans to a colander to drain. Return the water to a boil.

Remove the stems from the pumpkin leaves or spinach, then roughly chop the leaves. Add to the boiling water, reduce the heat, and simmer until very wilted, about 5 minutes.

Drain, rinse with cold water and drain again. Using a wooden spoon or potato masher, mash the pumpkin leaves or spinach to break them up a bit.

In a large pot, combine the mashed pumpkin leaves or spinach with the corn, green beans and potatoes. Add just enough water to cover, season with salt and bring to a boil. Reduce the heat to medium and simmer until the potatoes are tender and most of the liquid has been absorbed, about 20 minutes. If there is any liquid left, drain it off and discard. Using a wooden spoon or potato masher, mash the mixture until very smooth.

Meanwhile, in a large frying pan, heat the canola oil over medium-high heat. Add the scallions and cook, stirring, until golden, 5 to 7 minutes.

Add the mashed potato mixture and mix well. Season with salt, sprinkle with more scallions and serve hot.

3 cups (480 g) fresh corn kernels

3 cups (330 g) roughly chopped green beans

2 cups (45 g) pumpkin leaves or spinach

3 pounds (1.3 kg) russet or Yukon gold potatoes, peeled and halved

Salt

1 tablespoon canola oil

1 bunch scallions, finely chopped, plus more for serving

PESCADO CON PATACONES
Fish and Fried Green Plantains

Miguel Flaco
Embera Quera Community
Panama

Yield: 4 servings
Active time: 30 minutes
Total time: 1 hour

7 tablespoons fresh lemon juice (from 2 to 3 lemons), plus lemon wedges, for serving

1½ teaspoons annatto (achiote) paste

3 garlic cloves, minced

Salt

4 (5-ounce / 140 g) sustainably sourced tilapia or other white-fleshed fish fillets, such as flounder or sole

4 green (unripe) plantains (about 7 ounces / 200 g each)

3 cups (720 ml) sunflower oil, for frying

½ cup (64 g) all-purpose flour

To peel the plantains: Cut both ends off the plantains. With a small, sharp knife, score the ridges of the fruit lengthwise, cutting just through the layers of the tough peel, not into the fruit. Work the tip of the knife and your thumb under the strips of peel to release them and strip them off. Trim off any remaining peel with your knife. As you peel the fruit, place it in the bowl of acidulated water (2 tablespoons lemon juice to 4 cups / 960 ml water) to keep it from browning.

Miguel Flaco is a member of the Embera Quera indigenous community in Panama. He cares deeply about biodiverse food because it has the ability to sustain not only his life, but the lives of his children and grandchildren. In this staple dish, Flaco typically pairs tilapia with patacones—salted green plantains—but he encourages swapping for any fish that is local to your region and under minimal environmental threat. For the most traditional way to enjoy this dish, serve it on a "bijao," or banana leaf, and eat it with a green salad.

In a small bowl, combine 5 tablespoons of the lemon juice, the annatto paste, garlic and 1 ½ teaspoons salt. Let stand for 5 minutes to soften the paste, then whisk well to dissolve the paste. Pour into a shallow glass or ceramic baking dish. Add the fish, turn to coat in the marinade, and let stand at room temperature for 15 minutes.

Peel the plantains (see note). Drain the plantains and pat dry with paper towels. Cut into 1-inch-thick (2.5 cm) slices.

Pour enough oil into a deep 12-inch (30 cm) skillet, preferably cast iron, to come about halfway up the sides. Place over medium-high heat and bring to 350°F (180°C) on a deep-fry thermometer. Line a sheet pan with paper towels and set it near the stove.

Working in batches, carefully add the plantain slices to the oil and fry, flipping halfway through cooking, until golden and crispy around the edges, 6 to 8 minutes total. Using a slotted spatula, transfer the plantains to the paper towel-lined sheet pan and let cool at room temperature. Return the oil to 350°F (180°C).

Preheat the oven to 225°F (110°C). Spread the flour in a deep shallow plate or pie pan. Line a second sheet pan with a rack. Be sure the oil has reheated to 350°F (180°C). In two batches, lightly dredge the fish in the flour, shaking off the excess flour. Carefully slip the fish into the hot oil and fry until golden and crispy, about 6 minutes. Transfer the fish to the rack and keep warm in the oven while finishing the patacones.

Be sure the oil has reheated to 350°F (180°C). Stand the plantains on end on the paper towels. Use the bottom of a glass or a jar to press each cooled plantain chunk to make a disk about ¼ inch (0.5 cm) thick. Working in batches, carefully return the mashed plantains to the hot oil and fry until crispy, 2 to 3 minutes total. Return to the paper towels to drain and season with salt. Serve immediately with the tilapia and lemon wedges.

ONION-POACHED MACKEREL WITH OKRA AND RED BELL PEPPERS

Rita Otu
Nigeria

Yield: 4 servings
Active time: 20 minutes
Total time: 40 minutes

Rita Otu is a creative and influential farmer, food justice advocate and public speaker from Uyo, Akwa Ibom State, Nigeria. Her academic background in International Development led her to focus her work on food security, the environment and women empowerment. As a voice for women in sustainable agriculture, Otu takes an interdisciplinary approach to tackling the challenges Nigeria faces around food security; she aims to improve the food system by teaching others in her community to cultivate and grow their own food as a way to encourage a healthier lifestyle. As a farmer, it is also important to Otu to protect soil health by promoting biodiversity and reducing waste. This satiating recipe is composed of biodiverse ingredients that are locally grown. Rich in vitamins, minerals and dietary fiber, the vegetables in this dish help to reduce the risk for cardiovascular disease and support the body's immune system.

2 (7-ounce / 200 g) sustainably sourced skinless mackerel fillets

Salt and freshly ground black pepper

2 white onions

1 tablespoon olive oil

2 red bell peppers, finely chopped

14 ounces (400 g) okra, trimmed and finely chopped

1 ounce (28 g) spinach, stems and any thick veins removed and leaves thinly sliced

Mashed potatoes, for serving

Generously season the fish with salt and pepper.

Cut 1 of the onions into thin slices and finely chop the other onion.

In a large frying pan, bring half the onion slices and 1 ¼ cups (300 ml) of water to a boil. Add the fish, cover and poach until slightly opaque and only partially cooked, 3 to 4 minutes. Remove the fish and onion slices from the pan, place in a bowl and set aside. Measure the poaching liquid and add more water as needed so you have 1 cup (240 ml). Set aside.

In the pan used to poach the fish, heat the olive oil over medium-high heat. Add the remaining onion slices and the bell peppers and cook until softened, 5 to 7 minutes. Add the okra and finely chopped onion and stir to combine with the other ingredients. Add the reserved poaching liquid and cook, stirring occasionally, until the onion is softened and the okra is tender, 10 to 12 minutes. Add the fish and the reserved onion slices and cook, gently stirring to slightly break up the fish until the fish is fully cooked and flaky, about 5 minutes. Add the spinach and cook, gently stirring, until wilted, about 1 minute. Season with salt and pepper.

Serve hot with mashed potatoes.

Zahra Abdalla
Iran and Sudan

Sheila Flaherty
Inuit Community
Canada

Mbali Nwoko
South Africa

Andrew Zimmern
United States

Zoe Adjonyoh
Ghana

Natacha Gomez
Haiti

Yana Tannagasheva
Shor Community
South-West Serbia, Russia

Mariah Gladstone
Blackfeet Nation Community
United States

Dũng Võ Ngọc and Thanh Vuong
Vietnam

Omer Eltigani
Nubian Community
Sudan

Aleida Robles
Kuna Community
Panama

Alma Roblin
France

Rachael Sintamei Yiaile
Maasai Community
Kenya

Miguel Flaco
Embera Quera Community
Panama

Rita Otu
Nigeria

II. Biodiversity

Biodiversity

Variety is indeed the "spice of life"—especially on our plates! Tasting the world through regional cuisine is one of the greatest joys of eating. Food lovers everywhere know the thrill of discovering a new-to-them ingredient, and diverse diets often pack a hefty nutritional punch alongside their exciting textures, colors and aromas.

As biodiversity (the variety of life on Earth) dwindles, our plates are at risk of homogenization . . . and there is more at stake than flavor.

Biodiversity can be imagined as a measure of Earth's natural richness. Just as society flourishes when diverse cultures thrive, the planet is at its best when diverse plants and animals live on and within it.

All life on Earth depends on the health of our ecosystems. Stable, healthy ecosystems produce nutrient-dense food, balance carbon in the atmosphere and provide safe homes for humans and other species. When ecosystems destabilize due to climate change, land clearing and other invasive human activities, they become less supportive. This erodes the very foundations of our economies, livelihoods, health and quality of life worldwide. Biodiversity loss is a direct threat to human wellbeing, and it's happening every day.

The relationship between biodiversity and the quality, quantity and accessibility of our food supply is intimate.

There are over 300 varieties of corn, and yet we rely almost exclusively on 5 of them. In fact, 90 percent of crop varieties have already disappeared from farms around the world in the last 100 years. There are 391,000 edible plant species, but more than half of the global food supply comes from just three crops: wheat, rice and maize. Farmers do not take the risk of growing indigenous vegetables, fruits and grains for fear of spoilage and low demand—and due to sizable subsidies put in place to incentivize growing staple crops that can be turned into animal feed, fuel and ultra-processed food items.

While diverse and regionally appropriate diets offer plenty of fiber, a variety of amino acids and a stellar micronutrient profile, reliance on monocrops often leads to nutrient deficiencies.

Small organisms that contribute to fertile soil and produce micronutrient-rich crops are disappearing as biodiversity dwindles, lowering food quality. Pollinator loss—for example, from bees which are increasingly at risk—threatens $577 billion USD in annual global crops, and pests are more prevalent in less biodiverse areas. One million species are now threatened with extinction, including 40 percent of amphibians and a third of marine mammals.

And it's not just food! Many medical and pharmacological discoveries are made by examining flora and fauna. Biodiversity loss may limit potential future discoveries that could save lives. Traditional plant medicines are estimated to be used by 60 percent of the world's population and, in some countries, are an essential part of the public health system. Agricultural biodiversity also provides the raw materials for goods, such as cotton and wool for clothing and wood for shelter and fuel.

Despite achieving unprecedented economic growth in the past 50 years, underlying societal inequalities persist. There is more than enough food for everyone, but more than 3 billion people cannot afford even the cheapest healthy diet. Children are particularly at risk: In 2019, at least 340 million children suffered from micronutrient deficiencies, both over- and under-weight. This "double burden" of nutritional risks keeps them from realizing their full potential for prosperity and productivity.

WHAT'S CAUSING THIS?

Simply put: humans.

Three-quarters of the land-based environment and about 66 percent of the marine environment have been significantly altered by human actions. (However, these trends have been less severe or avoided in areas held by indigenous peoples).

Land clearance for agriculture is the main cause of biodiversity loss. Urban areas have more than doubled since 1992; there are more mouths to feed and less green space on which to sustainably grow food to do so.

Warming temperatures, pollution, overharvesting, overfishing, hunting, poaching and invasive species migration due to habitat destruction all contribute to biodiversity loss as well.

The beauty of food systems solutions is that they are all interconnected: the efforts that will increase biodiversity will also minimize waste, improve health and counteract climate change.

Advocates of health and sustainability keep coming back to this theme: less meat, more locally produced food and stronger policies.

Better land-use regulations and subsidized sustainable farming practices like cover cropping, composting and agroforestry improve biodiversity from the soil up. Transformations led by inspired individuals and youth are crucial in the way we organize our economies and societies.

The recipes in this chapter highlight ingredients that are native to the authors' respective regions. They have a sense of place. With food and flavors, these recipes connect you to the history of the land and its people with every bite and encourage you to explore your own local options that may be hiding in plain sight.

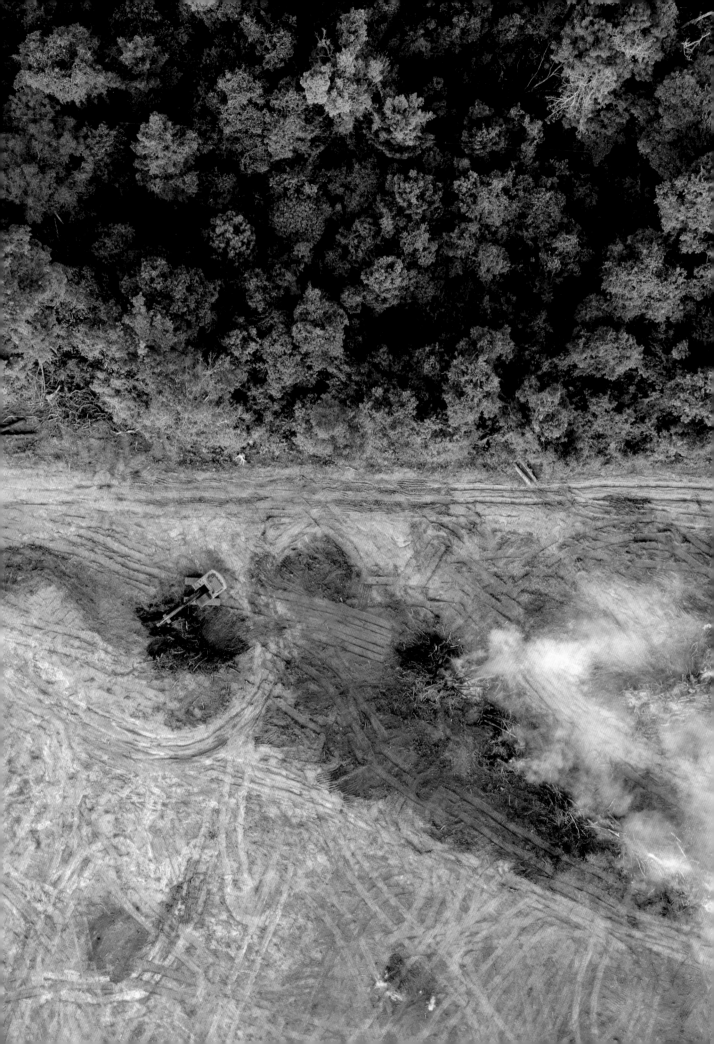

STINGING NETTLE TART WITH BREADNUT OLIVE OIL CRUST

Lyn Bishop
Panama

Yield: 8 to 10 servings
Active time: 40 minutes
Total time: 2 hours

Lyn Bishop is a free-spirited farmer and mentor who teaches others to "live the life you love." This mindset inspired Bishop to move to Chiriqui, Panama, to follow her dream of living a sustainable lifestyle close to nature. Her experiences have motivated her to develop nutritious recipes from local ingredients that are nearly forgotten yet still an important part of local tradition. "The plants and their history have rich stories to share with us, if we take the time to listen," insists Bishop. Globally, we see increases in cases of diabetes and hypertension due to diet, but by moving towards a more natural, sustainable way of farming, we can increase biodiversity in crop production and nutrient diversity in everyday diets to improve health outcomes. Bishop developed this nutritious tart using wild, often neglected plants harvested from her land, where she focuses on regeneration and soil health. She uses breadnuts to make the crust, but you can use ground almonds, chestnuts or hazelnuts.

For the crust:

1 cup (95 g) ground almonds (almond meal; not almond flour)

1 cup (128 g) all-purpose flour

¼ teaspoon salt

¼ cup (60 ml) olive oil

Nonstick cooking spray

For the topping:

1 tablespoon olive oil

1 white or yellow onion, chopped

2 ½ ounces (70 g) chopped stinging nettle or spinach

5 sustainably sourced large eggs

1 teaspoon Dijon mustard

1 teaspoon kosher salt

¼ teaspoon freshly ground black pepper

2 medium tomatoes, halved, cored and sliced

Chopped fresh chives, for serving

Make the crust:

Preheat the oven to 350°F (180°C).

In a medium bowl, whisk together the ground almonds, all-purpose flour and salt. Add the olive oil and ⅓ cup (75 ml) water and stir to combine. If the dough isn't coming together, add another tablespoon of water. Cover and refrigerate until firm, about 1 hour.

Spray a 9 x 13-inch (23 x 33 cm) baking dish with nonstick cooking spray. Press the dough into the bottom and ½ inch (1.25 cm) up the sides of the baking dish and bake until the edges start to brown, 25 to 30 minutes—if the dough puffs up, press it down with a spoon. Leave the oven on.

Meanwhile, make the topping:

In a large frying pan, heat the olive oil over medium-high heat. Add the onion and cook, stirring occasionally, until translucent, about 5 minutes. Add the stinging nettle and cook, stirring and adding a splash of water if the pan gets dry, until wilted, about 2 minutes. Remove from the heat and set aside.

In a medium bowl, combine the eggs, mustard, salt and pepper and whisk to combine.

Spread the nettle mixture very thinly over the prebaked crust then carefully pour the egg mixture over the vegetables. Arrange the tomato slices all over the tart. Set the baking dish on a sheet pan and bake until the eggs are set, 20 to 25 minutes.

Sprinkle with chives, cut into slices and serve hot or at room temperature.

BAKED SALMON WITH SUMAC, FENNEL AND FIGS

Daniel Boulud
France

Yield: 4 servings
Active time: 45 minutes
Total time: 45 minutes

2 shallots, sliced

5 ripe figs (4 halved and 1 diced)

1 cup (240 ml) red wine

Pinch of sugar

3 tablespoons unsalted butter

4 (½-pound / 225 g) pieces sustainably sourced center-cut, boneless, skinless salmon fillet (preferably Ōra King)

1 teaspoon sumac

¼ teaspoon fennel pollen

Salt and freshly ground white pepper

6 tablespoons (90 ml) olive oil

3 fennel bulbs (2 trimmed and each cut into eight small wedges; 1 trimmed and thinly sliced, preferably on a mandoline)

1 cup (240 ml) unsalted chicken broth or water

1 ½ teaspoons balsamic vinegar

1 handful arugula

1 to 2 tablespoons fresh lemon juice

French chef and restaurateur Daniel Boulud's childhood on a farm outside Lyon instilled in him the importance of equitable, sustainable food systems. That focus is evident in the cuisine he serves at his many restaurants around the world and in this recipe in which he pairs sustainably sourced salmon with locally foraged anti-inflammatory sumac, plump figs and thinly sliced fennel for an elegant, soulful dish. Boulud likes to use Ōra King salmon because of its sustainability properties, as well as its wide availability. It is also unlike other salmon, because it does not have to swim against the current, which attributes to a high fat content and unique marbling.

Set a rack in the center of the oven and preheat the oven to 350°F (180°C). Line a sheet pan with foil or a nonstick baking mat.

In a small saucepan, combine the shallots, diced fig, red wine and sugar and place over high heat. Cook until the liquid is reduced by two-thirds, 15 to 20 minutes. Strain through a fine-mesh sieve, discarding the shallot and fig, then return the liquid to the pan. Place over low heat and whisk in the butter. Keep warm.

Season both sides of the fish with the sumac, fennel pollen and ½ teaspoon salt. Drizzle with 2 tablespoons of the olive oil and arrange in a single layer on the prepared sheet pan. Bake until the salmon is fully cooked through and flakes easily when prodded with a fork, 7 to 8 minutes.

While the salmon is baking, in a medium saucepan, combine the fennel wedges, chicken broth and 1 tablespoon of the olive oil. Season with ½ teaspoon salt, place over medium heat and cook until the fennel is tender, about 6 minutes. Remove the fennel from the liquid and keep warm; discard any remaining broth.

In a nonstick medium sauté pan, heat 1 tablespoon of the olive oil over medium-high heat. Add the halved figs, cut side down. Reduce the heat to low, add the balsamic vinegar and cook, spooning the balsamic vinegar over the figs until they are lightly glazed, about 2 minutes. Remove from the heat and keep warm.

When ready to serve, toss together the arugula and shaved fennel and drizzle with the remaining 2 tablespoons olive oil. Drizzle with the lemon juice to taste and season with salt and white pepper.

Place the salmon onto warm dinner plates. Divide the braised fennel wedges and glazed fig halves among the plates. Arrange the arugula and shaved fennel on top of or next to the salmon, then drizzle the red wine sauce lightly around the plate and serve.

VENISON CARPACCIO WITH WATERCRESS SALAD

Grace Ramirez
Venezuela

Yield: 4 servings
Active time: 40 minutes
Total time: 1 hour

Grace Ramirez is a chef, cookbook author, activist and global TV personality from Venezuela. She is also part of a network of "Chefs for the People." As Chef Partner of the United Nations #ActNow campaign for sustainable food, which worked to tackle climate change one bite at a time, Ramirez joined Kitchen Connection and the United Nations International Fund for Agricultural Development to host a cooking session at the United Nations headquarters in 2019.

Ramirez's passion for sustainability is showcased in this recipe in which she highlights watercress, often coined "kale's underused cousin" and believed to be a highly underrated and underused vegetable by many in the culinary world. Not only can it add zest to salads, sandwiches, soups and sauces, but watercress also delivers twice as much vitamin C as an orange, along with fiber and potassium. When sustainably sourced, wild venison is considered a good source of protein. Venison is relatively low in fat and total calories while providing zinc and B vitamins.

1 ½ pounds (675 g) sustainably sourced boneless venison loin, fat and sinew removed

Fine sea salt and freshly ground black pepper

2 tablespoons avocado oil or ghee

4 garlic cloves, peeled and smashed

1 tablespoon Dijon mustard

4 tablespoons (60 ml) fresh lemon juice

6 tablespoons (90 ml) extra-virgin olive oil

2 avocados

2 (3 ½-ounce / 100 g) bunches watercress, roughly chopped

Flaky sea salt, for serving

Extra-virgin olive oil, for serving

3 ounces (85 g) hard-aged local cheese, shaved with a vegetable peeler (optional)

Generously season the venison with salt and pepper.

Heat a griddle or a heavy skillet large enough to hold the venison over high heat. Brush the avocado oil onto the hot griddle. Add the venison and sear, turning as needed, until brown all over, about 3 minutes total. Transfer the venison to a plate and let cool for 30 minutes.

Meanwhile, using a mortar and pestle, mash the garlic cloves with a pinch of salt until a paste forms. Add the mustard, 2 tablespoons of the lemon juice and the olive oil and whisk to combine. Season to taste with salt and pepper.

Thinly slice the avocados and drizzle with the remaining 2 tablespoons of lemon juice.

Using a very sharp knife, slice the venison loin across the grain as thinly as possible—aim for ⅛- to ¼-inch (0.25 to 0.5 cm) thick. Arrange the venison slices between sheets of plastic wrap and pound with a mallet or rolling pin until paper-thin.

In a large bowl, toss the watercress with the dressing. Season to taste with flaky sea salt.

Arrange the venison slices, slightly overlapping, on a large plate or platter. Drizzle with olive oil. Top with the watercress, followed by the avocado slices and shaved cheese, if using. Season with flaky sea salt and pepper as needed.

ADOBO BREADFRUIT WITH PICO DE GALLO

Sofia Castilblanco
Nicaragua

Yield: 4 servings
Active time: 45 minutes
Total time: 1 hour

For the adobo-marinated breadfruit:

½ cup (120 ml) fresh bitter orange juice (from 4 bitter oranges)

3 garlic cloves, finely chopped

1 teaspoon ground annatto (achiote seed)

1 teaspoon ground cumin

Salt and freshly ground black pepper

½ medium breadfruit, preferably mature but slightly underripe

2 tablespoons canola oil

For the pico de gallo:

2 tablespoons fresh lime juice

2 tablespoons apple cider vinegar

½ teaspoon ground cumin

6 medium tomatoes, diced

1 jalapeño, finely chopped (optional)

½ red onion, chopped

3 tablespoons chopped fresh cilantro (coriander) leaves

Salt and freshly ground black pepper

Sofia Castilblanco is a chef and food enthusiast from Managua, Nicaragua. Spending time in the kitchen of her mother's restaurant ignited her curiosity and passion for food, as well as concern for the planet. Given the impact of food on human and planetary health, Castilblanco believes that the key to a sustainable future is through an equitable food system in which there are more environment-friendly recipes to support it. This quick and easy recipe is inspired by traditional Nicaraguan adobo pork but is both vegan and plant-forward. Because it is not well-known and cooks typically do not know how to use it, breadfruit is often underutilized, but it is a nutritious and easy-to-prepare ingredient. With that in mind, Castilblanco created this simple yet enticing way to incorporate breadfruit into anyone's daily routine. Her adobo marinade can be used with cauliflower, potatoes, sweet potatoes or almost any vegetable. If you are unable to find bitter oranges, use 3 tablespoons (45 ml) orange juice and 5 tablespoons (75 ml) lime juice.

Marinate the breadfruit:

In a large bowl, combine the bitter orange juice, garlic, annatto, cumin and 1 teaspoon each of salt and pepper.

Peel the breadfruit and remove the core. Cut into roughly 1-inch (2.5 cm) cubes.

Fill a large bowl about three-quarters full with water. Add 2 teaspoons of salt and whisk to dissolve. Add the breadfruit and let stand for 3 minutes. Drain the breadfruit then add to the bitter orange juice mixture and toss to coat. Cover and let stand for at least 20 minutes.

While the breadfruit is marinating, make the pico de gallo:

In a large bowl, whisk together the lime juice, apple cider vinegar and cumin. Add the tomatoes, jalapeño (if using), red onion and cilantro and toss to combine. Season with salt and pepper.

Cook the breadfruit:

In a large skillet, heat the canola oil over medium heat. Add the breadfruit and sear, turning as needed, until all the sides have a golden-reddish color, about 15 minutes total. Serve with the pico de gallo.

NASI ULAM
Vegan Rice Salad with Homegrown Herbs

Azlin Bloor
Singapore

Yield: 6 servings
Active time: 25 minutes
Total time: 35 minutes

Azlin Bloor is a Singaporean chef and culinary instructor. A love of cooking is in her blood, and she hopes to make the world a better place for her children by emphasizing the importance of respecting all cultures, protecting the earth and improving our food system. Southeast Asia is home to nearly 15 percent of the world's tropical forest, but deforestation is causing severe biodiversity loss and harm to our environment in the name of agriculture. To counter this, Bloor grows as much as she can in her organic garden and conservatory, a tropical heaven for precious herbs, and then uses the food to make flavorful dishes like nasi ulam. This nutrient-dense vegan salad combines rice with homegrown herbs to create layers of color, texture and taste. It is a beautiful and special dish for sharing with friends and family but also perfect for quick weeknight meals.

Rinse the rice under cold running water. Drain the rice.

In a medium saucepan, heat the coconut oil over medium heat. Add the garlic and ginger and cook, stirring, for 15 seconds. Add the rice and toast, stirring constantly, for 1 minute. Add the coconut milk, pandan leaves, turmeric, 1 teaspoon salt and 2 cups (480 ml) of water; stir and bring to a boil over medium heat. Continue cooking the rice, uncovered, until all the liquid has been absorbed but the rice is not completely dry, about 4 minutes. You'll start seeing little holes on the surface. Stir the rice, cover and cook at a low simmer until the rice is cooked and nutty smelling, about 12 minutes more. Remove from the heat and let stand for 5 minutes.

Fluff the rice with a fork then transfer to a bowl. Add the herbs, scallions, tomatoes and red chili and stir to combine. Add the lime juice to taste, season with salt and pepper and serve.

If you prefer to serve this salad cool, let the rice cool completely before adding the remaining ingredients.

2 cups (360 g) long-grain white rice

1 tablespoon coconut oil or extra-virgin olive oil

3 garlic cloves, finely chopped

1 (1-inch / 2.5 cm) piece ginger, peeled and grated

1 cup (240 ml) coconut milk

2 fresh or frozen pandan leaves or 2 fresh or dried bay leaves

¼ teaspoon ground turmeric

Salt and freshly ground black pepper

1 ½ cups (60 to 75 g) finely chopped fresh herbs, such as cilantro (coriander), mint, Thai sweet basil (or regular basil), kaffir lime leaves, parsley, chives, tarragon or lemongrass (tough outer leaves, bulb and upper stalk discarded, and remaining stalk finely chopped)

2 scallions, finely chopped

15 cherry tomatoes, quartered

1 fresh red chili, such as bird's eye chili, finely chopped

2 to 3 tablespoons fresh lime juice

SEAFOOD OKRA

Michael Elégbèdé
Yoruba Community
Nigeria

Yield: 6 servings
Active time: 45 minutes
Total time: 1 hour and 10 minutes

(P)

¾ pound (340 g) sustainably sourced white, flaky fish, such as black sea bass, tilapia or fluke, cut into 2-inch (5 cm) pieces

½ pound (225 g) prawns or shrimp, deveined and shelled

¾ pound (340 g) cleaned calamari (squid), tubes sliced into ½-inch (1.25 cm) rings and tentacles roughly chopped

Salt and freshly ground black pepper

2 tablespoons vegetable oil

1 white onion, thinly sliced

2 red bell peppers, finely diced

2 fresh habanero chilis, minced

2 garlic cloves, minced

½ teaspoon freshly grated ginger

4 cups (960 ml) fish broth

1 tablespoon crayfish powder (ground crayfish)

1 teaspoon ogiri

½ teaspoon crushed uziza or freshly ground pepper

½ teaspoon baking soda

1 ½ pounds (675 g) okra, tops cut off and thinly sliced

Michael Elégbèdé is a Nigerian chef from Lagos. He is also a member of the Yoruba people, an indigenous group that is one of the largest ethnic groups in Nigeria. Elégbèdé's passion for food drives him to share his culinary creativity with the world in hopes of building a more sustainable food system for himself, his country and the world. Due to inadequacies in the storage and transport of fresh food, Nigeria suffers from the post-harvest loss of perishable, nutritious fruits and vegetables. In this recipe, Elégbèdé celebrates biodiversity and his Nigerian culture, while also supporting the health of people and the planet. His dish incorporates different types of fish and seafood, alongside shelf-stable ingredients that address the aforementioned transport and storage issues, thus reducing food loss. Depending on the fish you choose to use, you may need to cook it for more or less time. Ogiri can be found at an African market, which can also be a good source for uziza and dried crayfish powder, but if you have trouble finding either, swap in freshly ground black pepper and dried shrimp powder.

Place the fish, prawns or shrimp, and calamari in separate bowls, season with salt and pepper and set aside.

In a large pot, heat the vegetable oil over medium-high heat. Add the onion and cook, stirring, until translucent, about 3 minutes. Add the bell peppers, habanero chilis, garlic and ginger and cook, stirring, until the peppers are soft, about 5 minutes. Add the fish broth, increase the heat to high, and bring to a boil. Reduce the heat to medium-high and cook until the liquid is reduced by half, about 10 minutes. Add the crayfish powder, ogiri and uziza. Season with salt.

In a small bowl, whisk the baking soda and ¼ cup (60 ml) of water, then stir into the soup. Add the okra and simmer for 5 minutes. Season with salt. Add the fish and cook for 3 to 4 minutes, then add the prawns or shrimp and the squid and simmer until cooked through, about 3 minutes. Season to taste with salt. Serve hot.

SUSHI SALAAM

Bun Lai
Hong Kong

Yield: Makes 6 to 8 rolls
Active time: 2 hours
Total time: 2 hours

Bun Lai is a sustainability-focused sushi chef from Hong Kong who currently resides in Connecticut, in the Northeastern United States. As a chef, his goal is to create new ways of eating that encourage greater balance in the relationship between humankind and the rest of the living planet. Lai believes that the right to healthy food should be included in The Universal Declaration of Human Rights, because of the strong relationship between food and health. In his community of Woodbridge, many people face inadequate access to nutritious food options, an issue Lai attributes to government subsidies that incentivize the production of ultra-processed "junk" foods over healthier options. Lai created this vegan, "inside out" maki roll, which was awarded the 2016 White House Champion of Change Award for Sustainable Seafood. His dish is an homage to the cultures of the Middle East and defies the prejudice, bigotry and racism he sees on the rise, globally. By combining ingredients and flavors from the Middle East with Lai's own culture, this layered and delicate dish bridges cultural divides, while also incorporating a variety of biodiverse foods that help us collectively protect the Earth. In delicious bite form, it is an example of the peace and unity that can exist between people of different cultures and represents hope that we will one day live in a world without hatred and retribution.

For the lentils:
½ cup (103 g) French green lentils

For the sushi rice:
1 ¼ cups (258 g) white short-grain rice

¼ cup (48 g) brown rice

¼ cup (48 g) hulled barley

¼ cup (48 g) oat groats

¾ teaspoon ground turmeric

½ teaspoon freshly ground black pepper

¼ teaspoon ground mace

1 garlic clove, minced

1 tablespoon olive oil

2 cups (480 ml) pickle brine or vegetable broth

For the herb mixture:
1 bunch fresh flat-leaf parsley

1 bunch fresh cilantro (coriander)

1 bunch scallions, finely chopped

1 cup (35 grams) baby spinach, finely chopped

For the eggplant:
4 cups (960 ml) canola oil for frying

1 medium Italian eggplant (about 18 ounces / 500 g)

Salt

½ cup (60 g) all-purpose flour

For the sushi maki rolls:
1 (10-sheet) pack of full-sized nori sheets

¾ cup (96 grams) salted pistachios, roughly chopped, plus more for serving

2 medium carrots, cut into thin matchsticks

½ cup (75 g) dried figs, cut into very thin strips

½ cup (85 grams) pomegranate seeds (arils), plus more for serving

½ teaspoon ground cinnamon

Make the lentils:

Combine the lentils and 2 cups (480 ml) of water in a small pot over medium heat. Cover and cook until they have a snappy texture but are tender within, about 25 minutes. Drain the lentils in a sieve then rinse under cold running water for about 30 seconds to stop the cooking process. Let the lentils drain while you cook the rice mixture—you want the lentils to be as dry as possible before assembling the sushi.

Make the sushi rice:

Place the white rice in a large bowl, cover with cold water and swirl gently with your hand. Pour off any cloudy water, then rinse the rice in a fine-mesh sieve. Repeat this process a few times until the water is no longer cloudy. Transfer the washed rice to a medium saucepan. Add the brown rice, hulled barley and oat groats and stir to combine. Add the turmeric, pepper, mace and garlic and stir to combine. Add the olive oil and pickle brine or vegetable stock, 1 ¾ cups (300 ml) water and bring to a boil over high heat. Reduce the heat to low, cover and cook until the rice and other grains are tender throughout, about 15 minutes. Let stand, covered, for 20 minutes.

Make the herb mixture:

Set aside 8 sprigs each of parsley and cilantro. Remove the leaves from the remaining sprigs and finely chop them. In a large bowl, combine the finely chopped parsley and cilantro with the scallions and spinach. Measure ½ cup (about 45 grams) of the mixture and set aside.

Add the cooked rice to the herb mixture in the large bowl and gently stir to combine. Season to taste. Add the cooled lentils and gently stir to combine. Set aside.

Make the eggplant:

Fill a 3-quart or similar-sized saucepan with enough oil to come about 1 inch (2.5 cm) up the sides. Place over high heat and bring to 350°F (180°C) on a deep-fry thermometer. Line a sheet pan with paper towels and set it near the stove.

Peel the eggplant and cut it into sticks that measure about ½-inch-square (1.25 cm) and 2 to 3 inches (5 to 7.5 cm) long. Lightly salt the eggplant and then dust with flour.

Working in batches, carefully add the eggplant sticks to the hot oil and fry, turning as needed, until cooked through and golden brown all over, 1 to 2 minutes. Set on the paper towel–lined sheet pan to drain. Lightly season with salt.

Assemble the sushi maki rolls:

Cut two roughly 9 x 13-inch (23 x 33-cm) pieces of parchment paper and place one on a work surface. Arrange a nori sheet in the center of the parchment.

Moisten hands in water. Make a ball of rice approximately the size of a clementine and place it on the top half of your nori sheet. Use your fingers to spread the rice evenly so it covers the top half of the nori sheet. Make sure to cover all the edges well, so that your sushi roll does not collapse when rolled.

Spread pistachios on the top half of the rice, gently pressing it into the rice. Place the second sheet of parchment on top of the nori and use the two pieces of parchment to carefully flip the nori sheet, so the rice is now facing the work surface and you have the bare side of the nori facing you. Remove the top sheet of parchment and set aside.

Arrange a few of the reserved parsley and cilantro sprigs just above the middle of the nori sheet with the stems facing inward and the leaves facing outward so they will peek out of the ends. Spread about a tablespoon of the chopped herb mixture on the rice end of the nori sheet, then top with 4 sticks of fried eggplant, followed by 2 or 3 strips of the carrots and a few of the figs. Sprinkle with pomegranate seeds and finish with a sprinkle of ground cinnamon.

To roll your maki, take the empty half of your nori sheet and tuck it over and around the herbs and vegetables. Fold the parchment paper over and around the maki, then use your hands to gently squeeze the parchment-wrapped maki and shape it into a roll. Gently pull the parchment to release it from the maki. Continue using the parchment to roll and shape the maki until the seam of the nori is beneath the maki. Use your fingers to gently smooth out any bumps, then carefully remove the parchment. With a sharp knife, cut the maki roll into pieces. Repeat with the remaining ingredients to make more rolls. Sprinkle the rolls with pomegranate seeds and pistachios and serve.

MORINGA TEFF LASAGNA

Yohanis Hailemariam
Ethiopia

Yield: 4 servings
Active time: 40 minutes
Total time: 40 minutes, plus 45 minutes resting time

Chef and restaurateur Yohanis Hailemariam combines his innate creativity and Ethiopian heritage to serve healthy, African-inspired dishes both at his restaurant and on his cooking show. The growing population in Ethiopia necessitates food that is plentiful and native to the region. Ingredients that are locally produced like moringa, a nutritious herb that is originally from the Indian Himalayas but that now grows in Ethiopia, serve that purpose. This brightly colored lasagna also spotlights teff, a high-protein grain indigenous to Ethiopia.

Make the teff pasta dough:

In a large bowl, whisk together the teff and all-purpose flours. Tip onto a clean work surface in a large mound and make a well in the middle. Crack the eggs into the center of the well and add the olive oil. Beat the eggs and oil together with a fork and then begin mixing in the flour from the sides, gradually incorporating it into a single ball.

Dust a clean work surface with all-purpose flour and patiently knead the dough until smooth and elastic, 2 to 3 minutes. If the dough is too dry, add a couple drops of cold water as needed. Cover the dough with a clean kitchen towel and let rest for 30 minutes.

Dust the clean work surface again with all-purpose flour. Divide the dough into 8 equal-sized balls then press each ball into a flat disc. Using a rolling pin, roll the discs into very thin sheets. It's best to roll away from the center, stretching the dough outwards until it's the thickness of traditional lasagna sheets, ¹⁄₁₆ inch (1.5 mm) or thinner if possible.

Cut each stretched sheet into rectangular lasagna pieces, roughly 6 x 3 inches (15 x 7.5 cm). Arrange the sheets on clean kitchen towels, sprinkle with all-purpose flour and let dry for 15 minutes.

Fill a bowl with cold water and set by the stove. Bring a large pot of salted water to a rolling boil. Working in batches, add the pasta sheets one by one and gently cook, occasionally swirling the water to prevent sticking, until al dente, about 5 minutes. Transfer with a slotted spoon to the bowl of cold water to cool. Drain. Repeat to cook the remaining pasta.

Make the moringa bechamel:

In a saucepan, bring the milk to a gentle simmer, keeping a close eye so that it does not boil. Remove from the heat.

In a saucepan, melt the butter over medium-low heat. Add the flour, reduce the heat to low and cook, stirring, until it looks and smells a little toasted, 1 to 2 minutes. Gradually whisk in the hot milk and cook, stirring, until it thickly coats the back of a spoon, 1 to 2 minutes.

In a large sauté pan, heat the olive oil over medium heat. Add the garlic and cook, stirring, for 1 minute. Add half the moringa and cook briefly to wilt and make room in the pan then add the remaining moringa and season with salt. Cover and cook until the moringa is wilted and tender, about 5 minutes. Remove from the heat.

Place the moringa and bechamel in a food processor and blend until smooth. Season with salt and pepper.

Assemble and bake the lasagna:

Preheat the oven to 400°F (200°C). Grease the bottom and sides of a deep, 2-quart baking dish and place a layer of lasagna sheets across the bottom. Spread a thin layer of tomato sauce over the lasagna and then sprinkle with some of the mozzarella. Top with a thin layer of the moringa bechamel. Repeat this layering four times so that you have five layers of each ingredient, with the moringa bechamel on top.

Place in the oven and bake until the cheese has melted and the lasagna is cooked through, about 15 minutes. Season with pepper and serve hot.

For the teff pasta dough:

1 cup plus 1 tablespoon (165 g) teff flour

1 cup plus 1 tablespoon (136 g) all-purpose flour, plus more for rolling and dusting

3 sustainably sourced large eggs

1 ½ tablespoons olive oil

For the moringa bechamel:

1 ¼ cups (300 ml) whole milk

2 tablespoons unsalted butter

2 tablespoons all-purpose flour

1 tablespoon olive oil

1 garlic clove, roughly chopped

¾ pound (340 g) fresh tender moringa leaves or spinach, thick stems removed

Salt and freshly ground black pepper

For the lasagna:

1 ½ cups (360 ml) tomato sauce, preferably homemade

1 ¼ cups (175 g) grated fresh mozzarella

FRESH TUNA SALAD WITH HARISSA VINAIGRETTE

Einat Admony
Israel

Yield: 4 servings;
Active time: 20 minutes
Total time: 40 minutes

Einat Admony is an Israeli chef who believes that food is a means of connecting people by expressing love and unity, and that by protecting and improving the food system that we can provide a better future for our children and generations to come. Israel has seen an increase in diet-related non-communicable diseases, such as diabetes, obesity and heart disease, which Admony attributes to the fact that many people do not consume adequate daily amounts of fruits and vegetables. In this salad, she celebrates biodiversity by using locally sourced produce and freshly sourced tuna, but if sustainably sourced tuna and eggs are not available, either or both can be omitted to make this flavorful dish vegetarian or vegan. Admony's harissa recipe makes a lot, but it can be used on roast chicken or braised meats, as a spread for sandwiches or mixed with yogurt to make a dip.

For the salad:

4 large sustainably sourced eggs

2 large red potatoes (about 1 pound / 450 grams total), peeled and cut into ½-inch (1.25 cm) chunks

1 medium carrot, cut into thin matchsticks

2 teaspoons fresh lemon juice

Salt

2 preserved lemons (about 150 g total)

10 ounces (280 g) sustainably sourced solid white tuna (in oil or water), broken into chunks

½ cup (75 g) pitted manzanilla olives

Thinly sliced red onion, for garnish

Warm pita or challah, for serving

For the harissa vinaigrette:

3 tablespoons extra-virgin olive oil

3 tablespoons fresh lemon juice

2 to 3 tablespoons Homemade Harissa (recipe follows)

½ teaspoon honey

Salt

For the Homemade Harissa:

2 large red bell peppers

10 garlic cloves, peeled and smashed

1 ¼ cups (300 ml) canola oil

¼ cup (55 g) tomato paste

½ cup (40 g) ground cumin

⅓ cup (35 g) cayenne

⅓ cup (30 g) sweet Hungarian paprika

¼ cup (20 g) ground caraway

2 tablespoons kosher salt

Start the salad:

Fill a medium bowl with ice water. Bring a small pot of salted water to a boil. Carefully add the eggs and cook for 12 minutes. Use a slotted spoon to transfer the eggs to the ice bath and let cool completely. Once the eggs are cool, peel and cut into wedges.

Bring another small pot of generously salted water to a boil. Add the potatoes and cook until tender, about 10 minutes. Drain and let cool.

In a small bowl, toss the carrots with the lemon juice and a pinch of salt. Let stand at least 5 minutes.

Meanwhile, make the harissa vinaigrette:

In a large bowl, whisk together the olive oil, lemon juice, harissa and honey. Season with salt.

Finish the salad:

Thinly slice the preserved lemon then rinse under cold running water. Use a small sharp knife to remove the flesh and reserve for another use. Dice the peel. Add the diced peel, along with the potatoes, carrots, tuna and olives to the bowl with the harissa vinaigrette and toss to coat. Transfer to a platter; top with the eggs and a few slices of red onion. Serve with warm pita or challah.

HOMEMADE HARISSA

Makes about 2 ½ cups (490 g); active time: 20 minutes; total time: 1 hour

Preheat the oven to 450°F (230°C). Place the bell peppers on a sheet pan and roast, turning a few times, until the skins are completely wrinkled and the peppers are charred, about 30 minutes. Transfer the peppers to a bowl, cover tightly and let stand until cool enough to handle, about 20 minutes.

Once cool, remove and discard the stems from the peppers and cut each pepper into quarters. Remove and discard the peels, cores and seeds and place the peppers in a food processor. Add the garlic, 1 cup (240 ml) of the canola oil and the tomato paste and pulse until the mixture is almost puréed. Add the cumin, cayenne, paprika, caraway and salt. With the processor on, slowly drizzle in the remaining ¼ cup (60 ml) of canola oil and then continue processing until a thick paste forms. Refrigerate the harissa in an airtight container for up to 6 months.

SPICY OLLUCO WITH BEEF

Saturnina Kari Luna
Siusay Community
Perú

Yield: 4 to 6 servings
Active time: 15 minutes
Total time: 45 minutes

Saturnina Kari Luna is an indigenous farmer from the District of Lambrama, Province of Abancay, Apurimac, Perú. She is a member of the Siusay community and uses agroecological practices to enhance the nutritional value of the produce that she grows on her farm. Kari Luna's main motivation to improve the food system is for the improvement of the health of her family and her community at large. In Perú, extreme weather events caused by climate change, a decrease in biodiversity on farms and a disconnect between producers and consumers impacts food availability, consumer behavior and community nutrition. With this flavorful stew, Kari Luna spotlights olluco (also called molluco and ulloco), an underutilized crop that can be found frozen or canned at Latin markets. This one-pot dish is rich in nutrients, including calcium, phosphorus, vitamin B, vitamin C, iron and zinc, all of which promote good health for those within Kari Luna's community and for anyone who enjoys it. Kari Luna typically uses an herb called huacatay for garnish, but it is almost never found outside of Perú, so she suggests using a mix of herbs to achieve a similar flavor.

1 (1-pound / 450 g) bag frozen olluco slices (labeled olluco cortado; about 4 cups)

1 tablespoon vegetable oil

1 medium white onion, chopped

2 garlic cloves, minced

1 pound (450 g) sustainably sourced ground beef (preferably 80% lean ground chuck)

3 tablespoons ají panca paste

1 teaspoon sweet paprika

1 teaspoon dried oregano, crumbled

1 large ripe tomato, seeded and diced or 2 cups drained peeled canned tomatoes, coarsely chopped

1 large baking potato, peeled and cut into ¾-inch (2 cm) cubes

Salt and freshly ground black pepper

3 tablespoons chopped fresh flat-leaf parsley, basil, tarragon or mint leaves, preferably a combination

Put the olluco in a colander set in the sink and rinse under cold water to remove the frost. Drain. Set aside at room temperature until needed.

In a Dutch oven, heat the vegetable oil over medium heat. Add the onion and garlic and cook, stirring, until the onion is translucent and tender but not browned, about 4 minutes. Move the vegetables to one side of the pot and add the ground beef to the empty side. Increase the heat to medium-high and cook until the beef is beginning to brown, about 2 minutes. Stir the meat into the vegetables and cook, continuing to stir and break up the meat with a spoon, until it loses its raw look, about 5 minutes.

Stir in the ají panca paste, paprika and oregano. Add the tomato, potato and ½ cup (120 ml) of water. Mix well and bring to a simmer. Season with salt and pepper and bring to a boil. Reduce the heat to medium-low, cover tightly and simmer, stirring occasionally and adding more water as needed to keep the juices from sticking to the pot, until the potato is tender, 15 to 20 minutes.

If the olluco are sticking together, rinse and drain again then add to the pot, cover and cook until the olluco is hot and the stew juices are thickened, about 5 minutes. Season with salt and pepper. Divide among bowls, sprinkle with the fresh herbs and serve.

BUTTERNUT SQUASH LOCRO WITH QUINOA AND BRAZIL NUT CRUMBLE

Virgilio Martínez Véliz
Perú

Yield: 6 servings
Active time: 1 hour and 15 minutes
Total time: 1 hour and 30 minutes

For the butternut squash locro:

3 tablespoons canola oil

2 medium red onions, finely diced

4 garlic cloves

¾ cup (168 g) aji amarillo paste

Salt and freshly ground black pepper

1 medium butternut squash (about 38 ounces / 1060 g), peeled, seeded and cut into chunks

2 medium yellow potatoes, such as Yukon gold, peeled and cut into chunks

¾ cup (120 g) fresh or frozen corn

1 (12-fluid ounce / 354 ml) can evaporated milk

¾ cup (110 g) fresh or frozen peas

5 ½ ounces (154 g) fresh white cheese, such as queso fresco, crumbled

Fresh cilantro (coriander) leaves, for serving

For the Brazil nut crumble:

¾ cup (100 g) Brazil nuts, chopped

Salt

For the quinoa:

2 cups (340 g) white quinoa, rinsed

Salt

Chef and restaurateur Virgilio Martinez is at the forefront of the organic food movement in Perú, where he explores the region through his cuisine and research center, Mater Iniciativa. The organization is creating a registry of endemic flora species and meeting with Andean communities to rediscover lost herbs and ingredients. Martinez showcases Perúvian biodiversity in this beautiful golden-hued stew, served with quinoa, a crop that thrives in the high altitudes of the Andes mountains, and topped with bahuaja nuts (also known as Brazil nuts), which fall from the tallest and oldest trees in the Amazon. Aji amarillo paste is popular in Perú and makes this dish quite spicy; scale it back if you prefer less heat.

Make the butternut squash locro:

In a large Dutch oven, heat the canola oil over medium-low heat. Add the red onions and garlic and cook, stirring occasionally, until the onions are lightly browned, 15 to 20 minutes. Add the ají amarillo paste and cook, stirring, for 2 minutes. Season with salt and pepper. Add the butternut squash, potatoes, corn and 1 cup (240 ml) of water and bring to a boil. Reduce the heat, cover and simmer, stirring often to prevent sticking, until the squash and potatoes are tender, about 30 minutes. Add the evaporated milk, cover and simmer, stirring often and occasionally mashing the potato, until the potato falls apart and adds texture to the stew, about 20 minutes. Add the peas and cheese, stirring to incorporate and heat through. Season with salt and pepper and keep warm.

Make the Brazil nut crumble:

In a small frying pan over medium heat, toast the Brazil nuts, stirring, until golden, 4 to 5 minutes. Season with salt and remove from the heat. Transfer to a cutting board, let cool slightly and then chop into smaller pieces.

Make the quinoa:

In a small saucepan, bring the quinoa, a pinch of salt and 3 cups (720 ml) of water to a boil. Cover, lower the heat and simmer until a few of the grains start to uncoil and all the water has been absorbed, about 15 minutes. Remove from the heat and let stand, covered, for about 5 minutes. Fluff with a fork.

Divide the butternut squash stew and quinoa among bowls. Sprinkle with the Brazil nut crumble and fresh cilantro and serve hot.

FONIO AND SWEET POTATO CRAB CAKES WITH SPICY PAPAYA-LIME SAUCE

Pierre Thiam
Diola and Fulani Communities
Senegal

Yield: 4 to 6 servings
Active time: 45 minutes
Total time: 1 hour, plus 1 hour chilling time

Pierre Thiam is a Senegalese chef, restaurateur, author and social activist. He is a descendant of two major ethnic groups within Senegal—the Diola and Fulani people—and works to connect small farmers in Senegal to a larger marketplace by championing their nutritious and climate-resilient crops, like fonio (an ancient West African grain). More than one-third of the population in Senegal lives below the poverty line, which is partially due to climate change negatively impacting crops that are traditionally rain-fed. Thiam notes that the issue is exacerbated by farmers having limited access to processors and markets to sell the crops that they are able to grow. The fonio in Thiam's crab cake recipe encourages biodiversity by restoring soil health and producing a high yield under moisture-stressed conditions. This gluten-free grain is also a source of vitamins, minerals, fiber and the amino acids cysteine and methionine, which are not typically found in grains. Thiam suggests serving these crab cakes with a crisp and simply dressed green salad.

Make the crab cakes:

Bring a small pot of salted water to a boil. Add the sweet potato chunks, reduce the heat and simmer until tender and easily pierced with a fork, about 12 minutes. Drain the potatoes, place in a large bowl and mash with a fork until smooth. Let cool to room temperature.

Add the egg and egg yolk to the mashed and cooled sweet potatoes and beat with a wooden spoon until fully combined. Stir in the bell pepper, cooked fonio, cornmeal, scallion, parsley, lemon juice, mayonnaise, mustard, cumin and pepper. Fold in the crabmeat. Form the mixture into 12 cakes—they should be about 2 ½ inches (6.25 cm) in diameter and ½ inch (1.25 cm) thick—and sprinkle with the salt. Place on a platter, cover lightly with plastic wrap and refrigerate for at least 1 hour and up to 24 hours.

While the crab cakes are chilling, make the papaya-lime sauce:

In a blender, combine the papaya, Scotch bonnet chili, scallion, cilantro, lime juice, garlic and ¼ teaspoon salt. Process until the ingredients are fully combined but the mixture is still a bit chunky. Transfer to a small bowl, season to taste with salt and set aside.

Cook the crab cakes:

Line a large plate with paper towels.

Heat the vegetable oil in a large skillet over medium heat. Working in two batches, add the crab cakes and cook, flipping once, until golden brown all over, 3 to 4 minutes per side. Transfer to the paper towel–lined plate to drain. Repeat to cook the remaining crab cakes. Serve warm with the sauce and lime wedges on the side.

For the crab cakes:

1 large sweet potato (about 1 pound / 450 g), peeled and cut into 2-inch (5 cm) chunks

1 large egg plus 1 large egg yolk

1 green bell pepper, stemmed, seeded and finely chopped

½ cup (57 g) cooked fonio

¼ cup (34 g) finely ground cornmeal

1 scallion (white part only), chopped

2 tablespoons minced fresh flat-leaf parsley

2 tablespoons fresh lemon juice

2 tablespoons mayonnaise

2 teaspoons Dijon mustard

1 ½ teaspoons ground cumin

1 teaspoon freshly ground pepper

¾ pound (340 g) sustainably sourced lump crabmeat, picked over for cartilage and shells

½ teaspoon salt

⅓ cup (75 ml) vegetable oil

For the papaya-lime sauce:

1 cup (176 g) chopped peeled papaya

½ Scotch bonnet or habanero chili, stemmed, seeded and minced

1 scallion (white and light green parts), chopped

1 tablespoon chopped fresh cilantro (coriander) leaves

1 teaspoon fresh lime juice, plus lime wedges for serving

1 garlic clove, minced

Salt

SQUID WITH TOMATOES

Ivan and Sergey Berezutskiy
Russia

Yield: 4 servings
Active time: 15 minutes
Total time: 30 minutes

For the tomato broth:

6 ounces (170 g) tomatoes

For the warm tomato salad:

½ pound (225 g) tomatoes, sliced

½ pound (225 g) cherry tomatoes, halved

2 tablespoons extra-virgin olive oil

Salt and freshly ground black pepper

For the squid:

2 tablespoons unsalted butter

¾ pound (340 g) sustainably sourced squid (calamari), tubes sliced into ½-inch (1.25 cm) rings and tentacles roughly chopped

2 garlic cloves, minced

3 tablespoons fresh flat-leaf parsley leaves, chopped

2 teaspoons sour cream

1 tablespoon fresh basil leaves, chopped

3 tablespoons fresh cilantro (coriander) leaves, chopped

1 tablespoon extra-virgin olive oil

Identical twins Ivan and Sergey Berezutskiy are chefs in Moscow. They aim to introduce the diversity of Russian foods to the world through the art of cooking and source ingredients grown on farms in the immediate vicinity of their restaurant. In fact, the use of pesticide-free, locally grown, seasonal products is the cornerstone of their cooking and the reason they are able to produce such fresh and sustainable meals. By building a more sustainable food system, the Berezutskiy brothers hope to increase the consumption of foods that combat the high global prevalence of non-communicable diseases.

The Berezutskiy brothers usually make this dish with whelk, a typically underused shellfish and one they can source sustainably. However, if whelk is not available to you, use sustainably sourced squid as the recipe suggests. Fresh, lightly cooked tomatoes and a combination of garlic, parsley, basil and olive oil make this an easy, tasty, nutrient-dense meal that provides great flavors in addition to heart healthy omega-3 fatty acids. In summer, when tomatoes are at their peak, try to include a variety of colors and varieties for a truly eye-catching salad.

Make the tomato broth:

Preheat the oven to 350°F (180°C).

Spread the tomatoes on a sheet pan and bake until slightly softened, about 7 minutes. Press the tomatoes through a fine-mesh sieve set over a bowl. Discard the solids but reserve the tomato broth. Leave the oven set to 350°F (180°C).

Make the warm tomato salad:

Spread the sliced tomatoes and halved cherry tomatoes on a sheet pan, drizzle with the olive oil, season with salt and pepper and gently toss to combine. Bake until barely softened, about 4 minutes. Keep warm.

Meanwhile, cook the squid:

In a frying pan, melt the butter over high heat. Add the squid and fry, turning as needed, until lightly charred and cooked through, 4 to 5 minutes. Sprinkle with the garlic and parsley, remove from the heat and season with salt and pepper.

Arrange the warm tomato salad on a platter and top with the charred squid. Drizzle with the tomato broth, then dollop with sour cream and sprinkle with basil and cilantro. Finish with a drizzle of olive oil.

PAPEDA (SAGO PASTE) WITH FISH AND VEGETABLES

Hunanatu Matoke
Nuaulu Community
Indonesia

Yield: 4 to 6 servings
Active time: 15 minutes
Total time: 45 minutes

Hunanatu (Huna) Matoke is an indigenous member of the Nuaulu People who lives in Ambon, the capital city of the Indonesian province of Maluku. Her village traditionally ate sago, an underutilized starch from the spongy center of various tropical palm stems, because they were able to process it themselves even when money was tight. However, the typical Indonesian diet has shifted towards imported rice, which is more expensive and less environmentally friendly. By reintroducing sago paste, served with fish and vegetables in a turmeric-infused coconut sauce, Matoke seeks to return to more traditional meals to benefit the health of her people and the planet.

Make the fish in yellow sauce:

In a mortar and pestle, mash the red chilis, onions, garlic, lemongrass, ginger, galangal, turmeric and salt into a chunky paste. (Alternatively, combine the ingredients in a food processor and pulse until a chunky paste forms.)

In a wide, medium saucepan, heat the vegetable oil over medium heat. Add the chili paste and cook, stirring, until fragrant, 2 to 3 minutes. Add the coconut milk and lemon juice and bring to a simmer. Add the fish and mushrooms, cover and simmer until the fish is flaky, about 15 minutes. Add the papaya, stir and keep warm.

Make the papeda:

Bring 1 cup (240 ml) of water to a boil.

Meanwhile, in a very large bowl, mix the sago flour with ½ cup (120 ml) cold water, the lime juice and a pinch of salt. If the sago mixture is very thick, gradually add up to ¼ cup (60 ml) of additional cold water.

Pour the sago mixture through a fine-mesh sieve into a large bowl.

Add the boiling water and quickly whisk until it forms a clear paste and no white particles remain; it will be sticky.

Sprinkle the fish and vegetables with almonds and serve with the sago paste.

For the fish in yellow sauce:

5 to 10 fresh red chilis, finely chopped

2 white or yellow onions, finely chopped

2 garlic cloves, finely chopped

1 lemongrass stalk, tough outer leaves, bulb and upper stalk discarded, and remaining stalk finely chopped

1 (½-inch / 1.25 cm) piece ginger, peeled and grated

1 (1-inch / 2.5 cm) piece galangal, peeled and freshly grated

¼ teaspoon ground turmeric

1 teaspoon salt

⅓ cup (75 ml) vegetable oil

1 (13.5-fluid ounce / 398 ml) can coconut milk

1 tablespoon fresh lemon juice

4 (6-ounce / 170 g) sustainably sourced firm fish fillets, such as tuna, swordfish or halibut

½ pound (225 g) mushrooms, cut into small pieces

1 small green (unripe) papaya, peeled and cut into small pieces

¼ cup (27 g) finely chopped almonds, for serving

For the papeda:

1 ¼ cups (170 g) sago or tapioca flour

2 teaspoons fresh lime juice

Salt

CASHEW-CRUSTED FISH WITH CARAMBOLA SAUCE

Tita Inés Páez
Taíno Community
Dominican Republic

Yield: 4 servings
Active time: 35 minutes
Total time: 1 hour and 15 minutes

For the carambola sauce:

½ pound (225 g) star fruit (carambola)

2 tablespoons olive oil

1 tablespoon unsalted butter

½ white onion, finely chopped

1 (1-inch / 2.5 cm) piece ginger, peeled and grated

2 tablespoons orange liqueur, such as Cointreau

¾ cups (180 ml) strained star fruit (carambola) juice (from 7-star fruit)

1 tablespoon fresh lemon juice

¼ cup (50 g) sugar

Salt and freshly ground black pepper

For the fish:

Unsalted butter, for the pan

2 tablespoons coriander seeds

4 (¼-pound / 112 g) sustainably sourced skinless lionfish, cod or other firm, mild fish fillets

Salt and freshly ground black pepper

½ cup (66 g) cassava or tapioca flour

1 sustainably sourced large egg, lightly beaten

1 cup (124 g) finely chopped cashews, plus whole toasted cashews for serving

"Chef Tita" Inés Páez is an ambassador of New Dominican Cuisine. She was the first chef to focus her cooking on rescuing the gastronomic heritage of the Taíno indigenous peoples by sharing ancestral recipes of the Dominican Republic. In this dish, Chef Tita combines cashews with cassava, a staple of Taíno cooking, to create a crust for baked fish. Paired with a zesty carambola sauce, it makes for a sensational and nutritious meal that encourages biodiversity. To make the star fruit juice, you can purée chunks of fruit in a blender and strain it, or you can use a juicer.

Make the carambola sauce:

Trim the star fruit, then cut thin slices from the ends and set them aside for garnish. Chop the remaining star fruit.

In a medium saucepan, heat the olive oil and butter over medium heat. Add the onion and cook, stirring, until soft but not browned, about 8 minutes. Add the chopped star fruit and ginger and cook, stirring, for 1 minute. Add the orange liqueur and deglaze the pan, using a wooden spoon to scrape any bits off the bottom.

Add the star fruit juice, lemon juice and sugar; stir and cook until the sugar is dissolved, about 5 minutes. Transfer to a blender, place a kitchen towel on top and carefully blend until fully combined. Strain through a fine-mesh strainer, then return to the saucepan. Place over low heat and simmer until the sauce is thick and reduced by half, 15 to 20 minutes. Season with salt and pepper. Keep warm.

Make the fish:

Preheat the oven to 350°F (180°C). Butter a sheet pan.

In a small frying pan over medium heat, toast the coriander seeds until fragrant, about 3 minutes. Remove from the heat and let cool then use a mortar and pestle to finely crush the seeds.

Season the fish with salt and pepper.

Place the cassava flour and beaten egg in separate shallow bowls.

In a third shallow bowl, combine the crushed coriander with the finely chopped cashews. Season with salt and pepper.

Dredge the fish fillets in the cassava flour, then dip in the beaten egg. Repeat this process once more, then dredge the fish fillets in the cashew mixture. Place the fish on the prepared sheet pan and bake until the cashew crust is golden, 15 to 20 minutes.

Serve the fish with the carambola sauce and sprinkled with the reserved star fruit slices and whole toasted cashews.

Lyn Bishop
Panama

Daniel Boulud
France

Grace Ramirez
Venezuela

Sofia Castilblanco
Nicaragua

Azlin Bloor
Singapore

Michael Elégbèdé
Yoruba Community
Nigeria

Bun Lai
Hong Kong

Yohanis Hailemariam
Ethiopia

Einat Admony
Israel

Saturnina Kari Luna
Siusay Community
Perú

Virgilio Martínez Véliz
Perú

Pierre Thiam
Diola and Fulani Communities
Senegal

Ivan and Sergey Berezutskiy
Russia

Hunanatu Matoke
Nuaulu Community
Indonesia

Tita Inés Páez
Taíno Community
Dominican Republic

III. Sustainable Consumption

Eating Sustainably

"Tell me what you eat, and I will tell you what you are."

Jean Anthelme Brillat-Savarin

Any "foodie" can attest that food is more than just what we eat. In fact, our food choices have immediate health, environmental and ethical implications. Food can be a pathway to health or to disease; an expression of our policies, politics and culture; the sweat, effort, livelihoods and, too often, the exploitation of countless workers who grow, harvest, transport, process and prepare our foods. Unfortunately, today, the way we produce and eat food is the largest source of environmental degradation around the world, and it's putting the health of billions of people in jeopardy.

Consider a hamburger. When you see a quarter pound of beef sandwiched between buns and slathered in ketchup and mayonnaise—with a side of fries—you may not think much about health or the environment. But if you dig a little deeper, this meal can represent a lot more than what meets the eye: signs of heart disease or diabetes risk, increasing greenhouse gas emissions or Western culture seeping into every corner of the globe, changing what people aspire to eat.

Understanding *all* the roles food plays in our lives is important because it has a major impact on the health of both people and the planet. The foods most readily available and affordable—that hamburger and fries, for instance—are slowly killing us. In fact, unhealthy diets account for nearly 1 in 5 deaths worldwide. This trend isn't slowing down either. Obesity rates are rising with more than 1.9 billion people overweight or obese, including 38 million children under five. Not only is this tragic, but it also puts a huge strain on economies and the health system. People with diet-related diseases—diabetes, obesity, heart disease—are at greater risk for severe complications from common illnesses and unforeseen pandemics.

On the other side of the coin, hunger rates are increasing around the world. The nutritious foods that protect our health are unaffordable and inaccessible to many people. Our modern food system relies heavily on global imports and long supply chains—think shipping fruits from South America to the United States in the middle of winter or transporting produce from Asia to Africa and Europe. Distribution systems like this give us year-round access to fruits and vegetables we love, but they also make our food more vulnerable to disruptions, both close to home and far away. A political crisis or drought in one country can leave people on another continent hungry.

The food system is equally as disruptive to the environment. The food and agriculture sector accounts for an astounding 70 percent of global freshwater use and nearly one-quarter of all greenhouse gas emissions—that is more than every car, truck, ship, train and plane combined. The worst part is that all of this food production doesn't always lead to people with full bellies. The food system generates an overwhelming amount of waste. As much as one-third of all food grown is never consumed.

Our diet is destroying our bodies and the environment, and in order to make a change, we need to address the food system as a whole.

To understand what needs to change, it helps to understand how we got here. Today's food system was built to provide *more* food, but not *better* food. As large populations gathered in cities, and science and technology progressed, more of our food became mass produced, but further away from where people actually eat. More and more of our food has become mass produced, unlike in the early 1900s, when farms around the globe were small and isolated and the farmers' families often lived off their land.

The Green Revolution of the 1950s and '60s was a pivotal historical moment that led to a great increase in the production of rice, wheat and other grains. This movement lowered food prices and helped feed a billion people, but at the cost of an overwhelming amount of waste and increased greenhouse gas emissions. This shift depleted soil, water quality and natural habitats across the world and has led to some of the biggest environmental challenges we face today. Now, factory farms dominate agriculture systems in industrialized countries, using machinery and chemical fertilizers to produce more and increase profits. At the same time, smallholder farmers across the world are seeing their farms shrink in size, making it difficult to produce enough and earn a living.

Greater availability of cheap calories has not translated into more nutritious foods. What surrounds us in the supermarket or school canteen are often processed foods and beverages that are high in calories, unhealthy fats and sugars while, at the same time, low in vitamins and minerals. Further, producing these hyper-processed foods takes a bigger toll on the environment than their whole, unadulterated counterparts. An increased reliance on cheap, refined foods is harming our bodies and the planet.

Most people know that processed foods are bad—but it turns out some processed foods are worse than others. The food system puts the responsibility on consumers to educate themselves on the nutritional content and long-term effects of food on our health. However, the same system has conditioned them to habitually purchase processed or "junk food" because advertisers target children with colorful cereal boxes, cheerful jingles and cheap deals. A few countries have taken steps to solve this problem, and there are signs of progress. Parts of Mexico prohibit the sale of junk food to children, and the UK is planning to ban online and TV ads for unhealthy food.

It is clear that our global food system is failing to protect our health and the health of our planet. But it doesn't have to be this way. There are steps we can take toward healthy, sustainable and affordable food for everyone.

The first step is to take an honest look at what we eat. The latest science shows that healthy diets are composed of nutrient-dense foods like whole fruits, vegetables, nuts, seeds, legumes, whole grains and foods rich in omega-3 fatty acids (like fish or soybeans). They exclude ultra-processed items and are free from harmful additives. The foods that hold the key to improving human health are also critical in protecting the future of the planet.

We can question our favorite go-to meals. Many of us eat the same foods every day; it's easy and convenient but sadly deprives us of many health benefits. For our digestive system to flourish, it needs different vitamins, minerals and nutrients, and one of the best ways to accomplish that is to add color and diversity to our plates.

A simple way to promote gut diversity is to *eat the rainbow*. By filling our plates with different fruits and vegetables in a wide range of colors, we will naturally consume an array of important vitamins that prevent diseases and promote vitality. This book is full of delicious meals built on ingredients that, served together, offer that beautiful rainbow of nutritious colors. Regardless of your preferences—hearty or light, spicy or sour—there is a bounty of options that can spark kitchen creativity. We hope to empower every-one to make informed, healthy, safe and sustainable food choices—starting with you and your community.

Today, not everyone can access or afford the foods that support people and planet. Solving access issues requires big shifts that will transform our food system, such as governmental support for small farmers and food producers to grow nutritious food as opposed to the currently profitable refined grains and starchy vegetables. It will require spreading technology, like refrigeration and consumer data, so that fresh food can be delivered where it's needed and less goes to waste. And it will require helping big institutions like schools and hospitals buy and serve more nutritious meals. Understanding the changes needed transforms you from a reader to an advocate for more nutritious, equitable and sustainable food systems.

While we need to work together to create a "big picture" transformation of the food system in order to increase sustainable consumption, we still have the power to make small changes in the foods we eat, how much we consume and the amount of food wasted. Together, making small choices to eat nourish-ing food—for ourselves and the planet—will have a big impact.

Picking up this cookbook takes us one step closer to a tastier, healthier, more sustainable food future. Towards the back of the book, there are specific nutrition tips to inform choices that support your health goals while preserving our environment. We hope the ideas and recipes here inspire you to think about making your next meal not only delicious, but one that protects your health and the health of the planet.

PLANTAIN PURÉE

Ana Guerra
Zenú Community
Colombia

Yield: 4 to 6 servings
Active time: 25 minutes
Total time: 1 hour

Ana Guerra is the founder of Fundación Indígena Zenú de Bellavista in Colombia, which focuses on the sustainable development of the Zenú indigenous community. As a Zenú woman, Guerra works to support and empower women within her community by providing them with livelihood opportunities that help maintain their unique culture. Within the Zenú community, food sovereignty is of great importance. Guerra believes that indigenous communities have the inherent wisdom and knowledge to address climate change, but calls for partnership, understanding that no one group can combat this crisis alone. Guerra's recipe offers a simple way to showcase plantains, a crop that has long been grown at the homes of the Zenú women. Traditionally, this purée would be served on banana tree leaves, which make eco-friendly reusable plates that reduce waste. Though typically served at breakfast, plantain purée can be paired with fish, as shown here, or organic cow or goat's milk cheese to create a satisfying meal that can be enjoyed any time of day.

Juice of 1 lemon

4 large plantains or 5 green (unripe) bananas (about 23 ounces / 650 g total)

Salt

2 tablespoons lard

1 medium red onion, finely chopped

2 garlic cloves, minced

Fill a large bowl about three-quarters full with water. Squeeze the lemon juice into the water.

Cut both ends off plantains. With a small, sharp knife, score the ridges of the fruit lengthwise, cutting just through the layers of the tough peel, not into the fruit. Work the tip of the knife and your thumb under the strips of peel to release them and strip them off. Trim off any remaining peel with your knife. As you peel the fruit, place it in the bowl of lemon water to keep it from browning.

Bring a large pot of salted water to a boil over high heat. Add the peeled plantains, reduce the heat to medium, cover and cook until tender all the way through (the plantains should be soft enough to mash), 25 to 30 minutes. Transfer the plantains to a medium bowl; reserve the cooking water. Mash the plantains with a potato masher or fork until as smooth or chunky as desired.

In a medium frying pan, warm the lard over medium heat. Add the red onion and garlic and cook, stirring occasionally, until soft, about 5 minutes. Add to the mashed plantains, stirring to combine. If the purée is too dry, add some of the reserved cooking water, 1 tablespoon at a time. Season with salt and serve hot.

CHORBA WITH ROASTED EGGPLANT AND SWEET POTATOES

Nargisse Benkabbou
Morocco

Yield: 6 servings
Active time: 20 minutes
Total time: 45 minutes

2 medium eggplants (250 g each), cut into 1-inch (2.5 cm) chunks

2 large, sweet potatoes (250 g each), peeled and cut into 1-inch (2.5 cm) chunks

5 tablespoons olive oil

Salt and freshly ground black pepper

2 onions, finely sliced

2 medium tomatoes, finely chopped

3 tablespoons tomato paste

2 teaspoons ground turmeric

4 cups (960 ml) vegetable broth

1 (14-ounce / 400-g) can chickpeas, rinsed and drained

3 ½ ounces (100 g) spaghetti, broken into 1-inch (2.5 cm) pieces

Chopped fresh flat-leaf parsley leaves, for serving

Nargisse Benkabbou is a Moroccan author and chef. With a passion for sharing her culture and cuisine, Benkabbaou aims to inspire people around the world to embrace Moroccan flavors and ingredients in the kitchen, as well as to promote a healthy, well-balanced diet. Eager to make it easier—and more delicious—to cook and eat more healthfully, Benkabbou's recipe introduces a variety of vegetables in a simple and flavorful way. One of the key spices in this dish, turmeric, is widely used in Moroccan cooking and known for its antioxidant properties. In addition to adding incredible color and taste to dishes, turmeric may help control inflammation and support the body's immune system.

Preheat the oven to 400°F (200°C).

In a large roasting pan, toss the eggplant and sweet potato chunks with 3 tablespoons of the olive oil. Season with salt and roast until tender, 25 to 30 minutes. Set aside.

Meanwhile, in a large pot, heat the remaining 2 tablespoons of olive oil over medium-high heat. Add the onions and cook, stirring occasionally, until the onions are soft but not browned, 5 to 7 minutes. Add the tomatoes, tomato paste, turmeric, vegetable broth and 2 cups (480 ml) of water and bring to a boil. Reduce the heat to medium-low, cover, and simmer gently until the flavors meld, 30 to 35 minutes. Add the chickpeas, increase the heat to medium-high and bring to a boil. Add the spaghetti, along with the roasted eggplant and sweet potato, and return to a boil. Reduce the heat to medium-low and simmer, uncovered, until the spaghetti is al dente, about 10 minutes. Season with salt and pepper, sprinkle with parsley and serve.

SWEET POTATO GNOCCHI WITH KALE AND WALNUT BASIL PESTO

Luciana Gencarelli
United States

Yield: 6 servings
Active time: 1 hour and 30 minutes
Total time: 1 hour and 30 minutes

Luciana Gencarelli is an Italian-American entrepreneur in the United States. Her passion for food and business stems from her Italian roots—her family made wine and tomato sauce every summer—and her childhood habit of selling random items from her room to her younger sister. Gencarelli believes deeply in the holistic healing power of food. With dietary sensitivities in mind, Gencarelli's goal is to create delicious and nutritious meals, snacks and desserts that are free of gluten and dairy but full of taste, so that everyone can enjoy them. Her vegan and gluten-free version of gnocchi and pesto is plant-forward and nutritious. The sweet potatoes offer a high concentration of vitamins A and C, potassium and manganese, while the pesto contains healthy fats from olive oil and walnuts.

For the gnocchi:

5 pounds (2.3 kg) sweet potatoes (about 6 medium sweet potatoes)

2 tablespoons ground flaxseed

6 tablespoons (90 ml) warm water

4 cups (400 g) oat flour, plus about ½ cup (50 g) more for dusting

4 teaspoons pink Himalayan sea salt

Olive oil, for drizzling

For the pesto:

4 cups (70 g) packed fresh basil leaves

2 cups (50 g) packed kale leaves

2 teaspoons pink Himalayan sea salt

½ cup (120 ml) extra-virgin olive oil

¼ cup (22 g) toasted walnuts

8 cloves garlic, chopped

1 cup (105 g) vegan "Parmesan," plus more for serving

Start the gnocchi by bringing a large pot of water to a boil. Add the sweet potatoes and cook until tender, about 35 minutes. Drain the sweet potatoes and let cool for about 15 minutes, then pull off and discard the skins. Mash the sweet potatoes with a masher or fork until smooth and then let cool completely.

To make the pesto, combine the basil, kale and 2 teaspoons of the salt in a food processor. Pulse 12 to 15 times until the basil and kale are finely chopped. While blending on low, drizzle in the olive oil. Scrape down the sides of the food processor. Add the walnuts and garlic and blend on low until fully incorporated. Scrape down the sides of the food processor again. Add the vegan "Parmesan" and pulse 4 or 5 times until fully combined.

In a small bowl, whisk the ground flaxseed with the warm water and set aside to thicken.

Bring a large pot of salted water to a boil then reduce the heat until the water is gently boiling. Drizzle the bottom of a covered bowl with a little olive oil and set near the stove.

On a clean work surface, sprinkle the mashed and cooled sweet potatoes with the oat flour and the remaining 4 teaspoons of salt. Make a well in the center and add the flax mixture. Use your hands to mix the ingredients until a dough starts to form. Knead the dough, sprinkling with additional oat flour if the dough is sticky, until a very smooth mound of dough is formed. The dough should not be sticky, bouncy or elastic.

Divide the dough into 16 equal portions. Roll each portion into a long rope that is just under ½ inch (1.25 cm) in diameter. Cut each rope into approximately 22 (½-inch / 1.25 cm) pieces.

Using a slotted spoon, transfer 15 to 20 gnocchi to the pot of gently boiling water, stirring once to prevent sticking. Gently boil until the gnocchi float to the surface of the water, about 2 minutes. Use the slotted spoon to transfer the cooked gnocchi to the prepared bowl and cover to keep warm. Repeat to cook the remaining gnocchi.

Once the gnocchi are cooked, add the pesto to the bowl and toss to coat. Serve hot, sprinkled with additional vegan "Parmesan."

Refrigerate extra pesto in an airtight container, covered with a thin layer of olive oil, for up to 3 days, or freeze for up to 1 month.

KADOO
Afghan Braised Squash with Garlicky Yogurt Sauce

Humaira Ghilzai
Afghanistan

Yield: 4 servings
Active time: 25 minutes
Total time: 45 minutes

3 tablespoons olive oil

4 garlic cloves, minced

3 tablespoons brown sugar

2 teaspoons ground turmeric

4 tomatoes (about 20 ounces / 560 g total), roughly chopped

1 cup (240 ml) vegetable broth

1 medium sugar pie pumpkin or butternut squash (about 38 ounces / 1060 g), peeled, seeded and cut into 3-inch (7.5 cm) chunks

1 cup (226 g) plain full-fat yogurt

½ teaspoon garlic powder

Salt

Pita or Afghan naan, for serving

Afghan food blogger Humaira Ghilzai tells stories of Afghanistan's rich culture and its people through delectable food. She focuses on supporting regenerative agriculture and translating her family's traditions for the modern kitchen. Her kadoo recipe presents a fun, easy and unexpected way to prepare winter squash. Kadoo is excellent served with pita bread or Afgan naan.

In a medium saucepan, heat the olive oil over medium-high heat. Add the garlic, brown sugar and turmeric and cook, stirring constantly so the garlic doesn't burn, until fragrant, about 1 minute. Add the tomatoes and cook, stirring, for 1 minute. Reduce the heat to medium-low and simmer until the tomatoes are saucy and reduce slightly, about 10 minutes. Keep warm.

Meanwhile, in a large frying pan with a lid, bring the vegetable broth to a boil over medium-high heat. Add the pumpkin or squash, cover and simmer for 5 minutes. Add the tomato sauce, cover and simmer on low until the pumpkin or squash is fully cooked and a fork can go through it easily, about 15 minutes. Season with salt.

In a small bowl, combine the yogurt and garlic powder. Season generously with salt. Top the pumpkin or squash with yogurt sauce and serve with pita or Afghan naan on the side.

TOM KHA
Galangal Soup with Tofu and Mushrooms

Melissa Asawachatroj
Thailand

Yield: 2 to 4 servings
Active time: 30 minutes
Total time: 45 minutes

Melissa Asawachatroj is a Thai chef, cooking instructor and entrepreneur from Bangkok, who also holds a master's degree in food studies. Food has always played a prominent role in Asawachatroj's life. She is committed to improving the food system through the power of mindful, natural cooking and consumption practices. Asawachatroj's passion is driven by compassion, love for community and a desire to help our planet. The Thai population struggles with food insecurity driven by climate change, which has negatively affected crop yields and impacted the nutrient quality of ingredients. This spicy, plant-forward soup incorporates many aspects of sustainability by focusing on fresh, nutritious foods that can be locally sourced and cooked with a variety of underutilized ingredients. It is also designed to be shared with friends and family as a traditional round table dish. When shared with others, this meal provides a whole-person approach to health: caring for mind, body, spirit, community and planet.

In a medium pot, bring the vegetable broth to a boil. Add the shallots, galangal and lemongrass. Reduce the heat and simmer, uncovered, for 30 minutes to flavor the broth.

Meanwhile, prepare other ingredients. Chop the mushrooms and tofu into bite-sized pieces. Slice the Thai chilies on a diagonal, retaining all or some of the seeds, depending on your preferred level of spice. Wipe the cutting board clean and then roughly chop the cilantro.

Remove the broth from heat. Strain into another medium pot or strain it into a bowl while you wipe out the original pot, then return the broth to the medium pot. Discard the galangal, lemongrass and shallots.

Place the broth over medium heat and then gently stir in the coconut milk, mushrooms and tofu. Add the coconut sugar, soy sauce, makrut lime leaves, Thai chilies and 1 teaspoon salt. Bring to a simmer and cook, stirring occasionally, for 5 minutes.

Divide the lime juice and chili oil among soup bowls. Add the soup, garnish with cilantro and serve with Jasmine rice on the side.

4 cups (960 ml) unsalted vegetable broth

5 shallots, diced

1 (4-inch / 10 cm) piece galangal, unpeeled and cut into ⅛-inch thick (0.25 cm) slices

2 stalks lemongrass, tough outer leaves, bulb and upper stalk discarded, and remaining stalk cut into 1-inch (2.5 cm) pieces

7 ounces (200 g) mixed mushrooms, such as shiitake, button, oyster or shimeji

1 (2-pound / 900 g) block firm tofu

8 fresh Thai chilies

¼ cup (6 g) fresh cilantro (coriander) leaves, for garnish

1 (13.5-fluid ounce / 398 ml) can coconut milk

3 tablespoons coconut sugar

2 to 3 tablespoons soy sauce

6 fresh or frozen makrut lime leaves

Salt

2 to 3 tablespoons fresh lime juice

2 tablespoons Thai chili oil

Cooked Jasmine rice, for serving

TANGERINE AND TURMERIC BRAZILIAN CHICKEN STEW

David Hertz
Brazil

Yield: 4 to 6 servings
Active Time: 1 hour and 20 minutes
Total Time: 1 hour and 45 minutes, plus 1 hour marinating time

1 tangerine or small orange

3 cardamom pods

1 tablespoon ground turmeric

2 ½ teaspoons whole allspice

2 teaspoons whole black peppercorns

2 teaspoons cumin seeds

1 teaspoon fennel seeds

1 (½-inch / 1.25 cm) piece ginger, peeled and grated

2 small fresh cayenne chilis, very finely chopped

2 ½ teaspoons honey

1 cup (240 ml) coconut milk

1 pound (450 g) sustainably sourced boneless, skinless chicken thighs, cut into 2-inch (5 cm) chunks

1 bunch fresh thyme

4 tablespoons (60 ml) olive oil

2 red onions, diced (reserve the skins)

1 leek (white and light green parts only), thinly sliced and well-washed

5 medium tomatoes, cored and diced

4 okra, thinly sliced

Salt

½ cup (21 g) finely chopped fresh cilantro (coriander) leaves, for serving

½ cup (25 g) finely chopped fresh parsley leaves, for serving

Cooked couscous, for serving

David Hertz is a Brazilian chef from Rio de Janeiro and founder of Gastromotiva, an organization advocating for a better global food system. When submitting this recipe, the first words Hertz chose to describe himself were, "I cook, I feed, I dream." This phrase embodies the passion he feels for helping humanity by connecting us through food. Hertz eats with the vulnerable, cooks for the underprivileged and serves compassion alongside his meals. He believes that people who cook and eat together, stay together—connecting their souls and fueling their bodies. Through these food-built interpersonal relationships, we can take action towards the goal of "Zero Hunger" by reducing malnutrition and food-related non-communicable diseases. By using a variety of spices in this recipe, Hertz creates a simple, flavorful, well-balanced meal that helps prevent these chronic conditions. Hertz prioritizes fresh ingredients that can be locally sourced, such as honey, okra and coconut milk, which come together in a nutrient-dense dish that supports local farmers and the planet.

Zest the tangerine, then remove and discard the remaining peel. Cut the fruit into segments and reserve for the garnish.

In a mortar and pestle, crush the cardamom, turmeric, allspice, peppercorns, cumin seeds and fennel seeds until finely ground with no large pieces left. Add the tangerine zest, ginger, cayenne chilis and honey and mash until a smooth paste forms, about 5 minutes. Gradually add ¼ cup (60 ml) of the coconut milk, stirring to incorporate. Transfer to a large bowl, add the chicken and thyme, and stir to coat the chicken in the marinade. Cover and refrigerate for 1 hour.

In a large, deep frying pan, heat 1 tablespoon of the olive oil over medium-high heat. Remove the chicken from the marinade (discard any remaining marinade and the thyme), add to the pan and cook, stirring, until browned, about 4 minutes. Transfer the chicken to a plate; do not wash the pan but use a spoon to scrape off any remaining marinade. Add 1 tablespoon of the olive oil, along with the onions and leek, and cook over medium heat, stirring, until soft, about 4 minutes. Increase the heat to high, add the tomatoes and cook, stirring, until they break down and release their juices, about 5 minutes. Return the browned chicken to the pan, add the remaining ¾ cup (180 ml) of coconut milk and the reserved onion skins and bring to a boil. Reduce the heat to medium-low and simmer, uncovered, until the chicken is cooked through and the stew is fragrant, about 25 minutes.

While the stew is simmering, fry the okra. Heat the remaining 2 tablespoons of olive oil in a small frying pan over medium-high heat. Add the okra and fry until crispy and dark brown, about 5 minutes. Using a slotted spoon, transfer the okra to a paper towel to dry.

Remove and discard the onion skins from the stew, then generously season it with salt. Sprinkle the stew with the crispy okra, tangerine segments, cilantro and parsley. Serve with couscous on the side.

RED LENTILS AND BULGUR
Mjadra Hamra

Sara Assi
Lebanon

Yields: 6 servings
Active time: 45 minutes
Total time: 1 hour

Sara Assi is a dynamic home cook from Beirut, Lebanon. She studied dietetics and shares family-friendly recipes that are bursting with flavor and local Mediterranean ingredients like fiber-rich lentils and bulgur. In Beirut, these ingredients are often the most affordable, which means Assi's recipes make health-supportive eating accessible to all. This vegetarian meal is the epitome of Lebanese cooking—bright, textural and nutritious.

Make the lentils and bulgur:

In a large, wide pot, heat the olive oil over medium-high heat. Add the onions and 1 teaspoon salt and cook, stirring frequently, until the onions are dark brown, about 30 minutes. Add the lentils, cumin and ½ teaspoon pepper and stir to combine with the onions. Add the hot water and bring to a boil. Reduce the heat to low, cover and simmer until the lentils are soft, 20 to 25 minutes.

Rinse the bulgur in a fine-mesh strainer and drain well. Add the bulgur and 1 teaspoon salt to the onion and lentil mixture, stir well, cover and remove from the heat. Let stand for 10 minutes.

To serve:

In a large bowl, whisk the olive oil and lemon juice until fully combined. Add the lettuce, tomato, cucumbers and oregano and toss to combine. Season with salt and pepper.

Serve the lentil and bulgur mixture with the salad, yogurt, radishes, olives, pickles and pita.

For the lentils and bulgur:

⅓ cup (75 ml) olive oil

3 large white onions, finely chopped

Salt and freshly ground black pepper

2 cups (400 g) whole red lentils (or brown lentils), washed and drained

½ teaspoon ground cumin, or more to taste

5 ½ cups (1.3 liters) hot water

1 cup (160 g) coarse whole wheat bulgur (preferably #3)

For serving:

½ cup (120 ml) extra-virgin olive oil

3 tablespoons fresh lemon juice

6 cups (250 g) shredded romaine lettuce

24 cherry tomatoes, halved

3 kirby cucumbers, cut into thin rounds

3 tablespoons fresh oregano leaves

Salt and freshly ground black pepper

Yogurt, radishes, olives, pickles and pita, for serving

SPANAKOPITA

Katerina Delidimou
Greece

Yield: 8 servings
Active time: 1 hour
Total time: 2 hours

1 pound (450 g) spinach, stems and any thick veins removed and leaves roughly chopped

3 tablespoons olive oil, plus about ½ cup (120 ml) for brushing

2 medium yellow onions, chopped

Salt and freshly ground black pepper

5 scallions, thinly sliced

1 bunch fresh dill, finely chopped

½ cup (100 g) medium bulgur (preferably #2)

3 sustainably sourced large eggs, beaten

1 pound (450 g) feta, crumbled

1 (1-pound / 450 g) package phyllo dough

Katerina Delidimou is an Athenian food blogger who brings her love of traditional Greek cooking to family tables around the world. She has been virtually introducing the global community to Greek dishes beyond baklava for over a decade! Delidimou's beloved spanakopita features a crispy phyllo crust wrapped around vitamin-rich greens and tangy feta cheese. It can be served as a standalone dish or as part of a larger Mediterranean spread.

Place the spinach in a large bowl; set aside.

In a large frying pan, heat the 3 tablespoons of the olive oil over medium heat. Add the onions and a pinch of salt and cook, stirring often, until tender, 6 to 7 minutes. Add the scallions and cook until starting to wilt, about 2 minutes. Remove from the heat and stir in the dill and bulgur.

Scrape the onion mixture into the spinach and stir well until fully combined. Add the beaten eggs and the feta. Season with salt and pepper and mix well, using your hands as needed to thoroughly combine the ingredients.

Set a rack in the lower third of the oven and preheat the oven to 350°F (180°C).

Brush a 9 x 13-inch (23 x 33 cm) or similar-sized baking dish with olive oil.

Divide the package of phyllo dough in half. You will use one half to line the baking dish and the other half to go on top of the filling. The sheets are about the same dimensions as a 9 x 13-inch (23 x 33 cm) baking dish. As you are working, keep the phyllo covered with plastic wrap or wax paper then a clean kitchen towel. It helps to brush with oil then arrange the phyllo sheets.

Brush a phyllo sheet with olive oil and place crosswise on one side of the baking dish, so the ends hang over two sides. Brush a second sheet of phyllo and place it crosswise on the other side of the baking dish, so it overlaps slightly with the first sheet of phyllo and hangs over two sides. (If a sheet tears or wrinkles, simply place another on top.) Brush a third sheet of phyllo and arrange lengthwise in the baking dish and perpendicular to the first two sheets of phyllo. Continue to brush and layer in the same fashion until the base phyllo is gone.

Gently spread the spinach filling in the dish, leaving a ½-inch (1.25 cm) border on the short sides of the dish.

Using the other half of the phyllo sheets, brush each sheet with olive oil and then place lengthwise on top of the filling, brushing and layering until all the phyllo is used. Tuck the phyllo down and around the filling on the short ends of the dish where you left a ½-inch (1.25 cm) border to seal the spanakopita. Wrap any phyllo that is hanging over the sides of the dish on top of the final layer of phyllo, folding it as needed to seal the spanakopita and make a pretty edge. Brush the top layer once more with olive oil then cut the top layer of the phyllo into 12 or 16 squares, so it will be easier to cut later. Bake until golden, 50 to 60 minutes. Serve warm.

BEAN AND BELL PEPPER CHILI WITH CAULIFLOWER RICE

Gunhild Stordalen
Norway

Yield: 4 to 6 servings
Active time: 30 minutes
Total time: 1 hour and 25 minutes

Gunhild Stordalen is the Founder of EAT, a science-based global platform that aims to transform the global food system. As a medical doctor, public speaker, scientist, global leader and advisor to many international organizations, Stordalen works to link climate change, health and sustainability issues to build a fair and sustainable food system for healthy people and a thriving planet. Norway has a very cold climate with a short growing season, which means that growing and producing fresh food is difficult and expensive. This flavorful vegetarian chili is one of Stordalen's favorite home-cooked meals. The shelf-stable rice and beans provide a sustainable and affordable source of protein, while the vegetables and spices complement the dark chocolate, adding a powerful punch of flavor and antioxidants. Adjust the amount of fresh chilis and dried chili powder to suit your heat preference.

In a large Dutch oven, heat 2 tablespoons of the canola oil over medium-high heat. Add the onion, red and green bell peppers and a pinch of salt and cook, stirring often, until the onion and peppers are soft, about 10 minutes. Add the garlic, fresh red chili, cinnamon stick, coriander, cumin, paprika and chili powder and cook, stirring, until fragrant, 1 to 2 minutes. Add the mushrooms, toss to coat in the spices and cook, stirring, for 2 minutes. Add the diced tomatoes and their juices, the vegetable broth, tomato paste, brown sugar and a generous pinch of salt. Bring to a boil and then cover, reduce the heat to medium-low and gently simmer for 10 minutes. Add the kidney beans and continue gently simmering for about 30 minutes to heat the beans and thicken the chili slightly.

Meanwhile, make the cauliflower rice. Working in batches as needed, in a food processor, pulse the cauliflower until it resembles rice or couscous-sized granules.

When the chili is done, in a large frying pan, heat the remaining 2 tablespoons of canola oil over medium-high heat. Add the cauliflower rice and cook, tossing often, until heated through and browned in some places, about 5 minutes. Season with salt and pepper.

Just before serving, remove the cinnamon stick from the chili and add the chocolate. Sprinkle with fresh cilantro and more chocolate and serve with the cauliflower rice and yogurt or sour cream on the side.

4 tablespoons (60 ml) canola oil

1 large white onion, cut into large chunks

1 red bell pepper, cut into large chunks

1 green bell pepper, cut into large chunks

Salt and freshly ground black pepper

2 garlic cloves, finely chopped

1 to 2 fresh red chilis, finely chopped

1 small cinnamon stick

1 teaspoon ground coriander

2 teaspoons ground cumin

2 teaspoons paprika

2 to 3 teaspoons chili powder

½ pound (225 g) cremini mushrooms, halved

1 (14.5-ounce / 425 g) can diced tomatoes and their juices

1 ¾ cups (420 ml) vegetable broth

2 tablespoons tomato paste

1 tablespoon brown sugar or honey

2 (14-ounce / 400 g) cans red kidney beans, drained and washed

1 head cauliflower, trimmed and cut into florets

1 ½ ounces (42 g) dark chocolate (at least 70%), grated or finely chopped, plus more for serving

Chopped fresh flat-leaf cilantro (coriander) leaves, for serving

Yogurt or sour cream, for serving

SCALLION TARTE TATIN

Gaëlle Bonnieux and Claire Diquet
France

Yield: 4 servings
Active time: 20 minutes
Total time: 1 hour

14 thick scallions

5 tablespoons (70 g) unsalted butter

½ cup plus 1 tablespoon (135 ml) balsamic vinegar

4 teaspoons sugar

⅛ teaspoon red pepper flakes

Salt

½ pound (225 g) frozen puff pastry, thawed

Crumbled feta cheese or crème fraiche, for serving

Finely chopped fresh chives, for serving

Gaëlle Bonnieux and Claire Diquet are French farmers who run a female-powered farm that focuses on soil regeneration. They hope that their work sets a precedent for innovative and profitable farms and inspires a new generation of farmers to "grow" creatively. Over time, Bonnieux and Diquet have noticed an increase in poverty-related food insecurity, with the French population unable to achieve the recommendations for fruit and vegetable intake and adolescents drinking more carbonated drinks than the rest of Europe. To combat this trend, Bonnieux and Diquet dedicate themselves to cooking meals that are supportive of human health. This stunning vegetable tart can be made with affordable, easily accessible ingredients that provide dietary fiber and support human health. It also includes balsamic vinegar, which helps with digestion and can assist with regulating blood pressure.

Preheat the oven to 350°F (180°C).

Bring a large pot of water to a boil.

Trim the scallions. Then cut them roughly in half where the white turns to green—you should end up with roughly 8-inch (20 cm) pieces.

Submerge the scallion whites and greens in the boiling water and cook until soft, 3 to 4 minutes. Drain and set aside.

In an 8- to 9-inch (20 to 23 cm) oven-safe frying pan, melt the butter over medium heat. Add the vinegar, sugar and red pepper flakes. Season with ¼ teaspoon salt and cook for 2 to 3 minutes to slightly reduce the vinegar.

Arrange the scallions in rows in the pan and cook without stirring until the vinegar is reduced to a syrup, 10 to 15 minutes. Remove from the heat.

Cut the sheet of thawed puff pastry into a circle just slightly larger than the frying pan—reserve the scraps for another use. Carefully arrange the puff pastry on top of the scallions, tucking the edges into the pan. Bake until the pastry is golden brown, 20 to 25 minutes.

Place a serving plate on top of the pan and carefully flip it over so the pan is on top. Remove the pan. Top the tart with a dollop of crème fraiche or crumbled feta. Sprinkle with chives, cut and serve.

SOPA DE MILHO
Brazilian Corn Chowder

Denise Browning
Brazil

Yield: 4 servings
Active time: 20 minutes
Total time: 45 minutes

Denise Browning is a Brazilian chef and recipe developer who blogs about easy, healthy, budget-friendly recipes that are an ode to her heritage. Because drought is a common problem in parts of Brazil, Browning makes this traditional soup with locally available vegetables that require minimal transport and resources to produce. Creamy and comforting, her corn chowder is an instant classic that is elevated by a pop of color and aroma from chopped chives. You can use heavy cream or coconut milk in place of the yogurt.

In a large heavy pot, heat the vegetable oil over medium heat. Add the onion and cook, stirring, until softened and translucent, about 4 minutes. Add the garlic and cook, stirring, for 1 minute. Add the broth, increase the heat to medium-high and bring to a boil. Add the potato and 2 ¼ cups (360 g) of the corn, then reduce the heat and simmer until the potato is tender, 15 to 20 minutes. Season with salt and pepper.

Working in batches as needed, transfer the soup and some of the yogurt to a blender. Place a kitchen towel on top of the blender and carefully blend until creamy. Repeat as needed with the rest of the soup and yogurt. (Alternatively, add the yogurt to the pot of soup and use an immersion blender.) Return the soup to the pot, add the remaining 1 cup (160 g) of corn and cook, stirring occasionally, until the corn is cooked and hot, about 2 minutes. Season generously with salt and pepper. Divide the soup among bowls and garnish with chopped chives.

3 tablespoons vegetable oil

1 large white onion, chopped

4 garlic cloves, minced

6 cups (1.4 liters) low-sodium vegetable broth

1 large potato, peeled and diced

3 ¼ cups (520 g) fresh or frozen sweet corn

Salt and freshly ground black pepper

½ cup (113 g) plain full-fat yogurt

3 tablespoons chopped fresh chives

KERA NA CUTLETS
Banana Croquettes with Amaranth

Anahita Dhondy
India

Yield: 6 to 8 servings
Active time: 1 hour and 30 minutes
Total time: 2 hours and 30 minutes

4 large unripe (green) bananas (about 2 ¼ pounds / 1 kg total), washed but unpeeled

3 tablespoons sesame oil

5 to 6 hot green chilis, finely chopped

1 (1-inch / 2.5 cm) piece ginger, peeled and grated

1 teaspoon cumin seeds

1 teaspoon ground coriander

½ teaspoon ground turmeric

½ teaspoon ground cumin

2 tablespoons finely chopped fresh mint leaves

2 tablespoons finely chopped fresh cilantro (coriander) leaves

1 cup (200 g) cooked millet

¼ cup (60 ml) fresh lemon juice

Salt

1 cup (200 g) amaranth

Chutney, for serving

Anahita Dhondy is an Indian chef from Gurgaon, Haryana, who grew up surrounded by food. Her passion for cooking and her kitchen skills were ignited by her mother, who ran a catering business from home. As a large portion of the Indian population suffers from severe hunger and undernutrition, Dhondy hopes that she can use her work to share knowledge that will bring positive change to people's eating habits and provide more nutritious food for all. In this beautiful vegan dish, she flavors banana with a fragrant blend of spices including coriander, turmeric and both whole and ground cumin. She then adds millet and shapes the mixture into croquettes, or cutlets, that are rolled in puffed amaranth and baked. The result is a healthy, playful dish that supports our people and our planet.

Bring a large pot of water to a boil. Add the unpeeled bananas and cook until very soft—the bananas will turn black and the peels may split—about 45 minutes. Remove the bananas and let cool slightly. While still warm, peel and mash the bananas.

In a large frying pan, heat the sesame oil over medium-high heat. Add the green chilis, ginger, cumin seeds, coriander, turmeric and ground cumin, and cook for 1 minute to release the flavors. Add the mashed bananas, stir and cook for 5 to 7 minutes to flavor the banana. Add the fresh mint and cilantro, followed by the cooked millet, and mix to combine. Add the lemon juice, season with salt and remove from the heat. Let cool slightly.

Wet your hands and shape the banana mixture into about 25 croquettes, roughly ½ inch (1.25 cm) in diameter and 2 inches (5 cm) in length.

Preheat the oven to 350°F (180°C).

Heat a deep frying pan over medium-high heat.

Working in batches, add just enough amaranth to cover the bottom of the pan with a single layer. Cover the pan and shake it back and forth over the heat. You should hear the amaranth popping; if you don't, the pan isn't hot enough. As soon as the popping stops—this should take about 8 minutes—transfer the puffed amaranth to a sheet pan and let cool. Repeat as needed to pop all the amaranth. Set aside a small handful of puffed amaranth for serving.

Brush the croquettes with a little water and then roll them in the puffed amaranth and arrange on a sheet pan. Bake until the amaranth forms a crust, 35 to 40 minutes. Sprinkle with the reserved puffed amaranth and serve hot with chutney on the side.

SHULBATO
Cooked Bulgur with Eggplant, Peppers and Tomatoes

Rawia Bishara
Palestine

Yield: 8 servings
Active time: 1 hour
Total time: 1 hour and 15 minutes

Rawia Bishara is a Palestinian chef and restaurant owner. She uses food to connect the storied history of her people with a sustainable future by focusing on ingredients that are simple, local and delicious. Bishara's shulbato recipe comes from summers spent in her father's native village of Tarshiha, where sun-ripened vegetables and first harvest wheat were used to create this effortless, flavorful dish.

Preheat the oven to 425°F (220°C).

Place the eggplant in a colander, generously sprinkle with salt and let drain for about 30 minutes.

On a sheet pan, toss the zucchinis with ¼ cup (60 ml) of the olive oil and season with salt and pepper. Push the zucchini to one side to make room for the chilis. Place the chilis on the other side of the sheet pan and roast, stirring the zucchini occasionally, until the zucchini is tender and the peppers are browned and soft, about 20 minutes.

Rinse the eggplant, then squeeze it in a towel to remove excess moisture. On a sheet pan, toss the eggplant with ¼ cup (60 ml) of the olive oil and season with salt and pepper. Roast until tender, about 10 minutes.

Once the chilis are cool enough to handle, cut them about the same size as the zucchini and eggplant. Keep the vegetables warm.

In a large stockpot, heat ¾ cup (180 ml) of the olive oil over a medium-high heat. Add the onions and cook, stirring, until golden brown, about 10 minutes. Add the cumin and 1 tablespoon each of salt and pepper, followed by the bulgur, and stir until the bulgur is thoroughly coated. Add the diced tomatoes and cook until the tomatoes are soft, about 3 minutes. Stir in the tomato paste and cook for 1 minute. Add 4 cups (960 ml) of water, the chickpeas and half of the roasted vegetables. Bring to a boil, then reduce the heat, cover and simmer, stirring occasionally, until the liquid has been completely absorbed and the bulgur is tender but al dente, about 20 minutes. Season to taste with salt and pepper.

Transfer to a serving dish, top with the remaining roasted vegetables, drizzle with the remaining 2 tablespoons of olive oil and sprinkle with olives, if desired. Serve hot, cold or at room temperature.

1 large eggplant (about 18 ounces / 500 g), peeled and diced

Salt and freshly ground black pepper

3 medium zucchinis (about 1 ½ pounds / 675 g total), diced

1 ¼ cup plus 2 tablespoons (330 ml) extra-virgin olive oil

2 long hot chili peppers

2 white onions, diced

1 tablespoon ground cumin

3 cups (690 g) coarse bulgur wheat (preferably #4)

4 plum tomatoes, diced

2 (6-ounce / 170 g) cans tomato paste

1 (14-ounce / 400 g) can chickpeas, drained and rinsed

Black or green olives, pitted, for serving (optional)

SOPA DE LIMA
Yucatan Lime Soup

Alejandra Kauachi
Mexico

Yield: 6 servings
Active time: 20 minutes
Total time: 1 hour and 45 minutes

Chef Alejandra Kauachi is a proud and passionate Mexican cook dedicated to sharing the traditions and flavors of her ancestor's cuisine. She discovered her love for the culinary arts while growing up surrounded by the amazing spices and stories of her family's cultures. Typical Mexican diets include a lot of meat, including processed meat, and not enough fruits and vegetables to sustain health. Food insecurity is also a growing public health concern. Kauachi's soup highlights the flavors of Mexico and can easily be made with sustainably sourced chicken and vegetables to provide a warm feeling of home wherever it is enjoyed. You can use the more commonly available Mediterranean oregano for this recipe, but it is worth seeking out Mexican oregano, which has a more subtle, dusky flavor and can be found at Latin grocers (where you will also find the sweet peppers called ajis dulces).

6 large garlic cloves

1 teaspoon olive oil

2 (6-ounce / 170 g) sustainably sourced bone-in, skin-on chicken breasts

1 large white onion, chopped

1 large carrot, chopped

1 celery rib, chopped

2 fresh or dried bay leaves

8 whole black peppercorns

Salt

4 cups (960 ml) chicken broth

1 tablespoon dried Mexican oregano

2 cups plus 2 tablespoons (510 ml) vegetable oil

½ cup (40 g) seeded and finely chopped sweet peppers (ajis dulces) or green bell pepper

½ large tomato, seeded and chopped

⅓ cup (75 ml) fresh lime juice (from 2 to 3 limes), plus 1 lime, cut into 8 thin rounds

6 corn tortillas, cut into thin strips

Preheat the oven to 400°F (200°C).

Crush 2 of the garlic cloves under a knife but do not peel. Set aside.

Place the remaining 4 garlic cloves on a piece of aluminum foil and drizzle with the olive oil. Wrap the foil around the garlic and roast until the cloves are golden and completely soft when pierced with a knife, 40 to 50 minutes. Let cool then squeeze the garlic from the peels and set aside.

In a large saucepan, combine the chicken, the reserved 2 cloves of crushed garlic, half of the chopped onion, the carrot, celery, 1 bay leaf, 3 whole peppercorns and 2 teaspoons salt. Add about 8 cups (1.9 liters) of water to barely cover the chicken and bring to a boil over high heat. Reduce the heat to medium and simmer, occasionally skimming the foam off the surface, until the chicken is cooked through, 20 to 25 minutes.

Transfer the chicken to a plate and let cool; reserve the cooking liquid. Once the chicken is cool enough to handle, remove and discard the skin and bones and shred the meat into bite-size pieces. Set aside. Strain the cooking liquid, discarding the solids, then measure the cooking liquid and add enough chicken broth (about 4 cups / 960 ml) to come to 9 cups (2.1 liters) total. Set aside.

Meanwhile, make the garlic paste. Crumble the remaining bay leaf. Using a mortar and pestle, crush the crumbled bay leaf with the remaining 5 peppercorns and the oregano. Add the roasted garlic and mash into a paste.

In a large pot, heat the 2 tablespoons of vegetable oil over medium-high heat. Add the remaining onion, reduce the heat to medium and cook, stirring often, until soft but not browned, about 3 minutes. Add the sweet pepper and tomato and cook, stirring often, until the pepper is soft, about 3 minutes. Stir in the chicken broth mixture and the mashed garlic paste and bring to a boil over high heat. Reduce the heat to low and simmer for 15 minutes. Stir in the reserved shredded chicken and cook for about 1 minute, then remove from the heat and stir in the lime juice. Season with salt.

Meanwhile, make the crispy tortilla strips. Fill a medium frying pan with enough vegetable oil to come about ½ inch (1.25 cm) up the sides and place over medium-high heat. Line a sheet pan with paper towels and set it near the stove. Once the oil is shimmering, working in batches, scatter in the tortilla strips and fry until golden and crispy, about 30 seconds. Using a wire skimmer or slotted spoon, transfer the strips to the paper towel–lined sheet pan to drain. Ladle the soup into bowls, top with lime slices and crispy tortilla strips and serve.

SOUTH AFRICAN BOBOTIE

Theo De Jager
South Africa

Yield: 4 to 6 servings
Active time: 20 minutes
Total time: 45 minutes

Theo De Jager is a South African farmer and head of the World Farmers' Organization. On his farm, De Jager keeps goats and produces timber and subtropical fruits, including macadamia nuts, avocados and mangos. De Jager maintains that farmers are the backbone of our food system, as their labor provides the food we all eat, and they are key to helping us transition towards a more sustainable, resilient, nutritious and inclusive food system. In South Africa, stunting and wasting are major concerns. Food insecurity makes it difficult to meet children's nutrient needs, so De Jager relies on locally sourced meat that provides maximum protein and sustenance in his cooking. Here, he uses affordable and sustainable ground beef, but ostrich can be used instead. In fact, this dish is highly customizable and can be made with whatever fruits, vegetables and meat are found at your local farmers' market.

Make the bobotie:

Preheat the oven to 350°F (180°C). Brush an 8-cup (1.9 liter) or similar-sized baking dish with vegetable oil.

In a large, deep frying pan, heat the vegetable oil over medium-high heat. Add the onions and cook until soft but not browned, about 3 minutes. Add the beef and cook, stirring, until starting to brown, about 5 minutes. Add the curry powder and turmeric and cook, stirring, for 2 to 3 minutes. Add the jam and chutney and stir to combine. Reduce the heat to medium-low and simmer while you soak the bread.

In a medium bowl, briefly soak the bread in the milk then add both to the frying pan.

Add the raisins, almonds (if using) and the bay leaves and stir to combine. Cook for 2 to 3 minutes, then season with salt and pepper. Remove the bay leaves, then transfer the bobotie to the prepared baking dish.

In a small bowl, whisk together the eggs and cream, then pour over the bobotie and bake until the egg is cooked through and set, 20 to 30 minutes, depending on the baking dish.

While the bobotie is baking, make the rice:

In a small pot, combine the turmeric, salt and 2 cups (480 ml) of water. Bring to a boil, then add the rice and return to a gentle simmer. Cover and cook until the rice is tender, about 15 minutes. Remove from the heat and let stand, covered, for 2 to 3 minutes. Add the raisins, brown sugar and butter and stir to combine.

Garnish the bobotie with bay leaves and serve with rice, sliced bananas and chutney.

For the bobotie:

2 tablespoons vegetable oil, plus more for brushing the baking dish

3 small onions, chopped

18 ounces (500 g) sustainably sourced ground beef

3 tablespoons curry powder

2 tablespoons ground turmeric

¼ cup (68 g) apricot jam

½ cup (130 g) peach or mango chutney, plus more for serving

2 slices white bread, crusts removed

¼ cup (60 ml) whole milk

¼ cup (36 g) raisins or sultanas

2 ounces (56 g) sliced almonds (optional)

2 fresh bay leaves, plus more for garnish

Salt and freshly ground black pepper

4 sustainably sourced large eggs

¼ cup (60 ml) heavy cream

Sliced bananas, for serving

For the rice:

2 teaspoons ground turmeric

1 to 2 pinches salt

1 cup (180 g) long-grain white rice

¼ cup (36 g) raisins or sultanas

1 tablespoon brown sugar

1 tablespoon unsalted butter

Ana Guerra
Zenú Community
Colombia

Nargisse Benkabbou
Morocco

Luciana Gencarelli
United States

Humaira Ghilzai
Afghanistan

Melissa Asawachatroj
Thailand

David Hertz
Brazil

Sara Assi
Lebanon

Katerina Delidimou
Greece

Gunhild Stordalen
Norway

Gaëlle Bonnieux and Claire Diquet
France

Denise Browning
Brazil

Anahita Dhondy
India

Rawia Bishara
Palestine

Alejandra Kauachi
Mexico

Theo De Jager
South Africa

IV. Food &
Climate Change

Climate Change

A changing climate is nothing new. Planet Earth has always experienced "natural climate variability," or fluctuations in temperature that occur over long periods of time, without human interference. Volcanic eruptions, the Earth's orbit, and changes within the sun cause centuries-long weather events like ice ages, but our planet and its inhabitants have—for the most part—had time to adapt to those changes and survive.

Now, things are different. We are running out of time.

Between 2030 and 2050, climate change is expected to cause 250,000 additional deaths per year from malnutrition, malaria and heat stress.

Areas with weak health infrastructure—mostly in low- and middle-income countries—will be the least able to cope without humanitarian aid.

HOW DID WE GET HERE?

Global temperatures have been rising consistently since the Industrial Revolution of the 1800s sparked a technology boom. The past 30 years has accelerated warming even more: all of the top 10 worldwide warmest years on record have occurred since 1998. Increased industrial activity (including industrial agriculture) releases unprecedented amounts of gases that get trapped in the Earth's atmosphere, turning our planet into a giant greenhouse. This "greenhouse effect" causes relatively rapid increases in global temperature and more extreme weather events.

In the early 2000s, human-caused climate change impacted the likelihood or severity of 79 percent of all natural disasters. Hurricanes, blizzards, dust storms, flooding, tornados, erratic rain and heatwaves plunge communities into chaos and have lasting effects on human health.

As temperatures rise, delicate ecosystems like coral reefs and the Arctic become unbalanced and can be destroyed. Oceans acidify in warmer temperatures, threatening fish supply and coastal communities. This erasure causes biodiversity loss, which funnels our food consumption toward a narrowing group of foods that is not as health-supportive as a diverse diet.

Changes in ecosystems affect the livelihoods of farmers, fishers and nomadic communities; and when income suffers, so does people's ability to choose more nutritious food, which negatively impacts their health. Droughts can affect crop yields and ignite conflict as communities fight for the basic human resources of water and food. As animals are forced out of their natural habitats, they can "spill over" into human communities, accidentally introducing diseases.

Climate change has been identified as a key driver of food insecurity, which contributes to stunting, wasting and non-communicable diseases.

In our efforts to produce more food for our growing population, create profit and drive innovation, we have neglected our most precious resource: the planet.

HOW DOES THIS INVOLVE FOOD?

Our global reliance on ultra-processed foods delivered via long and unstable supply chains contributes to, and is influenced by, climate change.

Agricultural activities, from deforestation to food processing plants, make up about a third of greenhouse gas emissions. That is more than all of the cars, trucks, ships and planes combined! Half of the planet's arable land is dedicated to agriculture, and 30 percent of it is used to grow grain for animal feed instead of people. When food products are transported by plane, train and truck—all high emitters—their carbon footprint grows even larger.

Trees that help absorb carbon dioxide are plowed down to graze animals or grow cash crops to meet the demand for profits. Unconsumed food, tossed into landfills, continues to contribute to climate change creating methane (a greenhouse gas more potent than carbon dioxide) as it rots.

An unsustainable food system contributes to climate change . . . but as the climate changes, we must try harder to produce sustainable, local food.

HOW DO WE BREAK THE CYCLE?

We can start with questions that help us understand the journey of our food: Where is it grown? Who grew it? How did it get to my plate? As aware and empowered individuals, we can band together to insist upon more sustainable practices from farms and food companies and demand bold climate policy from our governments.

We can create fun opportunities for communities to connect with food from an early age at home and school. Learning about the connection between food, natural resources and their health will expose them to different cultures and equip them to be food systems advocates. You, the youth of our world, are the agents of change who are the best equipped to lead us—not just in food, but in all areas of sustainable technology and economy. You are plugged in and passionate and have a creative perspective on how to meet challenges within your communities.

We can shift to climate-positive diets (which happen to be excellent for human health) and inspire behavior changes within our families, workplaces and communities. The recipes that follow in this chapter are examples of those, averaging less than 50 percent of the carbon emissions of an average plate in the countries with the highest greenhouse gas emissions.

We can approach climate change issues with fresh eyes through partnerships across the sectors, working together for our common good without having "too many cooks in the kitchen."

We can restore degraded land, which would remove up to 51 gigatons of carbon dioxide from the atmosphere and raise food production by 17.6 megatons per year.

We can encourage technological innovations that help produce food with fewer inputs, transport existing food more effectively and increase food safety. Moreover, we can ensure that technological advances are shared equitably and serve those who need them most and that innovation efforts prioritize purpose over profit.

By committing to a climate-friendly food system, we can make healthier food more affordable and help people live longer, healthier lives . . . and we might just save the planet along the way.

Methodology for Carbon Footprint Calculations:

Assumptions and Data Sources

A carbon emissions calculator tool was developed for Kitchen Connection to provide cradle-to-farmgate emissions estimates for each recipe in this cookbook.

The 15 recipes featured in this chapter represent those with the lowest greenhouse gas emissions in the book. The estimates are in "kilograms of carbon dioxide equivalent" (kg CO_2e) and are representative of the emissions produced per serving of the recipe. Where servings represent a range, the lower servings estimate was used to determine the emissions per serving. These estimates include the greenhouse gas (GHG) emissions that are generated from the agricultural production of each ingredient found within the recipe. Cradle-to-farmgate emissions could include emissions from fertilizers used, methane from enteric fermentation of livestock and land use change, among other sources. Given the variability of these processes, emissions related to packaging, transportation, cooking methods and disposal of food were not included in these estimates but would surely increase the overall emissions.

DATA SOURCES

The GHG emissions data used in this cookbook are estimates sourced from the dataFIELD (database of Food Impacts on the Environment for Linking to Diets). This data was aggregated through extensive literature reviews and publicly available data on LCA (Life Cycle Assessment) research. In compiling emissions estimates for the cookbook's recipes, proxy ingredients were used when exact sources for recipe ingredients were not available.

As emissions from agricultural practices vary greatly across regions based on the growing methods used, these figures serve solely as estimates for the cookbook reader to conceptualize and better understand the environmental footprint of one's food choices.

According to research conducted in 153 countries, the average of dietary emissions associated with a full day of eating is 2.113 kg CO_2e per person.

To put this into perspective, 1 kg CO_2e is equivalent to 2.5 miles (or 4.02 km) being driven by an average passenger automobile.

Based on this figure, that breaks down to an average of .704 kg CO_2e emitted each meal. However, many developed countries' diets exceed planetary boundaries—either because of limited agricultural space in highly urbanized areas or demand for imported foods—resulting in higher emissions per meal than the global average. Of the 67 countries with the highest emitting diets (exceeding planetary boundaries by more than 10 percent), dietary emissions average 3.143 kg CO2e daily, or 1.047 kg CO2e per meal. That's a lot of carbon emission!

The median and average emissions calculations for the recipes in this cookbook are as follows: .43 kg CO2e (median) and .84kg CO2e (average), both of which are below the global average for the largest emitters listed above at 1.047 kg CO2e per meal. In fact, the median calculations for the emissions of the recipes in this book represent recipes that emit 58.9 percent less carbon than the global average per meal in the world's highest-emitting countries.

ON SIKIL BI BU'UL
Black Bean Pipian

Rosalia Chay Chuc
Mayan Community
Mexico

Yield: 6 to 8 servings
Active time: 15 minutes
Total time: 2 hours and 15 minutes, plus 8 hours soaking time

0.04 kg CO₂e This meal emits 96.18 percent less carbon than the average meal in the world's highest-emitting countries.

Indigenous chef and culinary advisor Rosalia Chay Chuc leads cooking classes that pass down traditional Mayan recipes in her hometown of Yaxuná, Yucatán. She learned to cook from her grandmother, making tortillas and using traditional underground ovens, and she now shares her passion for Mayan culture with travelers and visiting chefs. Her Sikil Bi Bu'ul is cost-effective, nutrient-dense and packed with flavor largely due to the addition of pipian, a pepita-based sauce, and recado blanco, a roasted garlic paste that can be used to flavor almost any soup or stew or as a rub for meat. Traditionally, this hearty dish is enjoyed with piping hot corn tortillas.

1 cup (190g) dried black beans, picked over and rinsed

1 large head garlic

1 teaspoon olive oil

⅓ cup (56 g) whole annatto seeds (achiote)

1 tablespoon dried Mexican oregano

½ tablespoon freshly ground black pepper

¼ cup (40 g) pepitas (toasted pumpkin seeds)

1 ½ teaspoons salt

Chopped red onion, fresh cilantro (coriander) and warm corn tortillas, for serving

In a large bowl, combine the black beans with enough room temperature water to cover. Let stand for at least 8 hours or overnight. Drain the beans and discard the water.

Preheat the oven to 400°F (200°C).

Peel any loose papery skins off the head of garlic, then cut about a ¼ inch (0.5 cm) off the top to expose the individual cloves. Place the head of garlic on a piece of aluminum foil and drizzle with the olive oil. Wrap the foil around the head of garlic, place on a sheet pan or in a small baking dish and roast until the cloves closest to the center are completely soft when pierced with a knife, 40 to 50 minutes. Let the garlic cool, then squeeze the soft garlic from the cloves into a bowl.

In a small bowl, combine the annatto seeds and 1 cup (240 ml) of room temperature water. Let stand until the seeds turn the water orange, about 15 minutes. Strain the liquid into another bowl and discard the seeds.

Using a mortar and pestle or molcajete, combine the roasted garlic with the oregano and pepper and mash into a paste. Measure 1 tablespoon and reserve any extra for another use.

In a blender or food processor, pulse the pepitas until finely ground. Add 1 cup (240 ml) of water and the 1 tablespoon of garlic paste and process until completely blended, about 1 minute.

In a large pot, combine the beans, pepita-roasted garlic mixture, the annatto soaking liquid, 2 cups (480 ml) of water, and the salt. Bring to a boil, reduce the heat and simmer, uncovered, until the beans are soft, about 1 hour. Season with salt. Serve hot topped with red onion and cilantro, and with warm corn tortillas on the side.

SWEET AND SOUR PUMPKIN

Niyati Parekh
India

Yield: 4 servings
Active time: 30 minutes
Total time: 45 minutes

0.05 kg CO₂e This meal emits 95.22 percent less carbon than the average meal in the world's highest-emitting countries.

Niyati Parekh is a professor of public health nutrition who works at the intersection of nutrition, chronic diseases and food environment in various settings and communities. Due to globalized food systems homogenizing consumption, many people are deficient in essential vitamins, which Parekh attempts to combat with this recipe. Pumpkin and squash are rich in beta-carotene, the carotenoid and antioxidant that gives squash its vibrant hue and that our bodies can convert into vitamin A. They are also a perfect way to showcase ingredients common in Parekh's native India, including ginger, coriander, chili powder, fennel, cumin, turmeric, tamarind and jaggery, an unrefined sugar you can find in Indian markets.

¼ cup (60 ml) vegetable oil

2 teaspoons black mustard seeds

1 (3-inch / 7.5 cm) piece ginger, peeled and grated

4 teaspoons ground coriander

2 teaspoons red chili powder, such as Kashmiri

2 teaspoons fennel seeds

2 teaspoons ground cumin

½ teaspoon ground turmeric

2 ¼ pounds (1 kg) winter squash, such as sugar pie, cheese pumpkin or butternut squash, peeled, seeded and cut into 1-inch (2.5 cm) chunks

2 tablespoons strained tamarind pulp (see note) or jarred tamarind concentrate

2 tablespoons crushed jaggery or brown sugar

Salt

Chopped fresh cilantro (coriander) leaves, for serving

Indian bread, such as roti, naan, puri or paratha, for serving

In a large saucepan or Dutch oven, heat the vegetable oil over medium-high heat until very hot but not smoking. Add the mustard seeds and cook until they start to pop, almost immediately. Add the ginger, coriander, chili powder, fennel, cumin and turmeric and cook, while stirring, to toast the spices without burning them, for 1 minute. Add the squash and cook, stirring to coat in the spices, for about 1 minute. Stir in 1 cup (240 ml) of water and bring to a boil over high heat. Reduce the heat to medium, cover, and cook at a brisk simmer, adding more water as needed, until the squash is tender and the sauce is thick and clinging to the squash, 8 to 10 minutes. Move the squash to one side of the pot and pour the tamarind in the empty area.

Add the jaggery and stir and crush to dissolve the jaggery. Gently mix the tamarind mixture into the squash mixture and cook, uncovered, to combine the flavors, about 1 minute. If the sauce seems too thick, stir in a few tablespoons of hot water. Season with salt. Sprinkle with cilantro and serve with the bread.

Note: To prepare tamarind pulp, cut a roughly 2-inch (5 cm) square from a block of tamarind paste. Coarsely break up the paste into a small bowl and add hot tap water to cover. Let stand about 5 minutes to soften the paste. Drain in a coarse wire sieve set over a bowl. Using a wooden spoon or your fingers, rub as much of the softened paste through the sieve as possible, being sure to scrape the bottom of the sieve. Discard the seeds and fiber in the sieve. Measure the 2 tablespoons pulp liquid for this recipe and reserve any remaining tamarind for another use. It can be refrigerated or frozen in an ice cube tray.

WHITE TEPARY BEANS AND NOPALES SALAD

Sean Sherman
Oglala Lakota Community
United States

Yield: 6 servings
Active time: 45 minutes
Total time: 2 hours and 45 minutes, plus 8 hours for soaking

0.06 kg CO$_2$e

This meal emits 94.27 percent less carbon than the average meal in the world's highest-emitting countries.

Sean Sherman is a chef, author, educator and founder of North American Traditional Indigenous Food Systems (NATIFS). As a member of the Oglala Lakota tribe, Sherman focuses his work on the revitalization and evolution of indigenous food systems across North America. He is well-known as an advocate for indigenous foods and works to educate others on the benefits of localized food systems. Nutritious food availability is a major concern within the United States, especially in Native American communities, so he hopes that popularizing low-resource indigenous ingredients will make food more accessible to all. In this delectable dish, Sherman demonstrates the ease of incorporating indigenous ingredients like tepary beans and dandelion greens into nutritious meals that can feed a crowd at low cost to the earth. Tepary beans are highly nutritious and worth seeking out at specialty shops or online. If you cannot find them, you can use any dried white bean, but adjust the cooking time accordingly, as tepary beans take longer to cook than most dried beans.

1 ½ cups (277 g) dried white tepary beans, picked over and rinsed

2 fresh nopales (cactus paddles; about 170 g each)

1 cup (17 g) fresh dandelion greens, cut into thin strips

½ small red onion, thinly sliced

3 tablespoons pure agave syrup

2 tablespoons sunflower oil

1 tablespoon Guajillo chili powder

1 tablespoon fresh oregano leaves, plus more for serving

1 teaspoon salt

In a large bowl, cover the beans with 5 cups (1.2 liters) of room temperature water and let soak overnight.

Drain and rinse the beans and place in a large pot. Add 7 cups (1.7 liters) of water and bring to a boil. Reduce the heat and gently simmer until the beans are tender, 2 to 2 ½ hours. Remove from the heat, drain, rinse with cold water and let cool.

Meanwhile, using a small, sharp knife, scrape all the thorns off both sides of the cactus paddles, then use the knife or a vegetable peeler to cut off the edges, going all the way around both paddles. Cut the cactus paddles lengthwise in half, then thinly slice each half crosswise. Place the cactus slices in a large pot, cover with cold water and bring to a simmer. Continue simmering, skimming any mucilage (it will look like the slime that comes off okra) until the cactus stops secreting it, about 5 minutes. Remove from the heat, drain and rinse with cold water.

In a large bowl, combine the cooled beans, cooled cactus slices, dandelion greens, red onion, agave syrup, sunflower oil, chili powder, oregano and salt. Toss to combine and sprinkle with more oregano. Serve room temperature or chilled.

145

BULGUR AND SPINACH WITH YOGURT AND POMEGRANATE

Manal Al Alem
Jordan

Yield: 6 servings
Active time: 15 minutes
Total time: 30 minutes

0.07 kg CO$_2$e

This meal emits 93.31 percent less carbon than the average meal in the world's highest-emitting countries.

1 cup (230 g) coarse bulgur wheat (preferably #4)

3 tablespoons olive oil

1 scallion (white and light green parts), chopped

2 garlic cloves, minced

1 teaspoon ground cumin

1 teaspoon ground coriander

1 teaspoon salt

¼ teaspoon ground cinnamon

¼ teaspoon freshly ground black pepper

1 tablespoon tomato paste

1 ½ cups (360 ml) boiling water

¼ pound (112 g) fresh spinach, chopped

Seeds (arils) from one medium pomegranate (1 ¼ cups / 215 g)

3 tablespoons pomegranate molasses or fresh lemon juice

Plain yogurt, for serving

Manal Al Alem is a chef from Jordan, and a Goodwill Ambassador for the United Nations World Food Programme. She shares recipes that can be made quickly and with minimal food waste in an effort to fight hunger worldwide and encourage proper nutrition from a young age. Beautifully garnished with ruby red pomegranate arils, her vegetarian salad is not to be missed.

Rinse the bulgur and drain.

In a medium saucepan, heat the olive oil over medium-high heat. Add the scallion and garlic and cook, stirring, until softened but not browned, about 2 minutes. Add the cumin, coriander, salt, cinnamon and pepper and cook for 1 minute. Add the bulgur, tomato paste, and boiling water and bring to a boil. Lower the heat, cover and simmer until the bulgur is tender, about 15 minutes. Transfer to a platter, add the spinach and toss to combine. Sprinkle with the pomegranate seeds, drizzle with the pomegranate molasses and serve with yogurt on the side.

BRAISED CUT KOMBU
WITH MUSHROOMS AND SHIRATAKI

Rina Matsuo
Ryukyu Community
Japan

Yield: 6 servings
Active time: 30 minutes
Total time: 1 hour and 30 minutes, plus 5 hours soaking time

 0.08 kg CO₂e This meal emits 92.36 percent less carbon than the average meal in the world's highest-emitting countries.

 V

Rina Matsuo is a Japanese chef from Naha, Okinawa, and a member of the Ryukyu indigenous community. She works to amplify Okinawan food culture, which is well known for promoting longevity. The traditional Okinawan diet also supports economic and environmental sustainability by focusing meals on locally grown and produced ingredients. Matsuo notes that the diet patterns of Okinawa have shifted recently with the influence of Western culture, and this has created poor health outcomes and food insecurity for people in the community. To return Okinawan cooking to its roots, Matsuo created this vegan dish starring two local ingredients that help support human health: shiitake mushrooms and kombu, an edible seaweed. Yam-based shirataki noodles are low in calories but soak up all the rich, umami flavor in this dish. They can be found at Asian markets or at well-stocked supermarkets.

1 ounce (28 g) dried shiitake mushrooms

2 ounces (56 g) dried kombu

1 tablespoon vegetable oil

2 carrots, peeled and cut into thin 2-inch (5 cm) long pieces

6 ounces (170 g) shirataki noodles, cut into roughly 2-inch (5 cm) long pieces

¼ cup (60 ml) soy sauce

3 tablespoons cooking sake

2 tablespoons sugar

1 tablespoon mirin

Salt

In a large bowl, soak the dried shiitake mushrooms in hot water for 5 hours; they will be very soft. Remove the mushrooms and chop if large. Set aside. Strain the soaking liquid through a fine-mesh sieve and set aside.

Fill a large bowl with cold water, add the kombu, and soak for 30 minutes. Remove the kombu from the water and gently pat it dry with a kitchen towel. Discard the water.

Cut the kombu into strips that are about 2 inches (5 cm) long and ⅛ inch (0.25 cm) wide.

In a medium saucepan, heat the vegetable oil over medium heat. Add the rehydrated mushrooms, the carrots and shirataki noodles, followed by the soy sauce, cooking sake, sugar and mirin. Cook, stirring, for 2 minutes. Using a slotted spoon, transfer the mushrooms, carrots and shirataki noodles to a bowl, leaving as much of the sauce behind as possible.

Add the strained mushroom stock and sliced kombu to the saucepan and bring to a simmer. Continue simmering until the sauce is reduced by half, about 30 minutes. Return the mushrooms, carrots and shirataki noodles to the pan, stir to combine and continue simmering until the carrots are tender, about 30 minutes. If the sauce reduces too much, add up to ½ cup (120 ml) of water. Season with salt. Serve hot.

"LA BANDERA" DOMINICANA
Dominican Rice and Beans

Gloria and Juana Hidalgo
Dominican Republic

Yield: 6 servings
Active time: 35 minutes
Total time: 2 hours, plus 4 hours soaking time

0.11 kg CO$_2$e This meal emits 84.49 percent less carbon than the average meal in the world's highest-emitting countries.

Gloria and Juana Hidalgo are Dominican restaurateurs who share their mother's legacy and culture through family recipes like this "La Bandera Dominicana," meaning the Dominican flag. Typically, this dish is accompanied with meat, but it is just as delectable without it. Beans already require less water than other protein sources to be produced, and the meatless version goes one step further by re-using some of the liquid from cooking the beans to make a flavorful sofrito. Beans also require less fertilizers to grow, thus reducing greenhouse gas emissions. Rice and beans have complementary properties: the amino acids in these ingredients are like pieces to a puzzle, fitting together to form a complete protein. The sofrito, used by the Hidalgos' ancestors to flavor their food, provides depth without processed additives or preservatives.

For the beans:

½ pound (225 g) dried pinto beans, picked over and rinsed

2 fresh sweet chilis, cored and halved

½ green bell pepper, cored and halved

1 garlic clove, minced

1 tablespoon olive oil

1 teaspoon salt

½ teaspoon dried oregano

2 bunches fresh cilantro (coriander), tied together with kitchen string

For the sofrito:

2 teaspoons olive oil

2 tablespoons finely chopped white onion

1 garlic clove, minced

½ teaspoon dried oregano

½ tablespoon salt

2 tablespoons tomato paste

1 teaspoon apple cider vinegar

For the rice:

1 ½ cups (270 g) long-grain white rice

1 tablespoon olive oil

1 teaspoon salt

Make the beans:

In a bowl, combine the pinto beans with enough room-temperature water to cover. Let stand for at least 4 hours or overnight. Drain the beans and reserve the water. Measure 1 cup (240 ml) of the water and set aside. Discard the remaining water or reserve for another use.

In a large pot, combine the beans with about 8 cups (1.9 liters) of water so they are completely covered. Add the chili peppers, bell pepper, garlic, olive oil, salt and oregano and bring to a boil over high heat. Reduce the heat to low, cover and simmer, stirring every 30 minutes, until the beans are tender and shedding their puffed layer when stirred, 1 ½ to 2 hours.

Meanwhile, make the sofrito:

In a small frying pan, heat the olive oil over medium heat. Reduce the heat to low. Add the onion, garlic, oregano and salt and cook, stirring continuously, for 1 minute. Add the tomato paste and apple cider vinegar and cook, stirring continuously, for 1 minute more. Remove from the heat and set aside.

Make the rice:

When there is about 40 minutes left to cook the beans, rinse and drain the rice. In a medium pot, heat the olive oil and salt over medium heat. Add 2 ½ cups (600 ml) of water, cover and bring to a boil over high heat. Add the rice and cook, stirring frequently to keep the rice from sticking to the bottom of the pot and lowering the heat as needed to maintain a gentle simmer, until most of the water has been absorbed, 20 to 25 minutes. Reduce the heat to as low as possible, cover tightly and continue to cook until the rice is almost dry, about 25 minutes. Remove from the heat and stir with a fork to fluff the rice.

When there is about 20 minutes left to cook the beans, but they are already tender, remove the peppers and place them in a blender. Add the sofrito and the reserved 1 cup (240 ml) of bean-soaking water to the blender. Blend until smooth and creamy, about 30 seconds. (Alternatively, use an immersion blender.) Add this mixture to the pot of beans. Pick a few leaves off the cilantro and reserve for serving. Add the rest of the cilantro to the beans and cook, stirring occasionally, until the sauce is smooth and creamy, but the beans still hold their shape, 15 to 20 minutes. Remove the tied cilantro. Serve the beans over the rice, sprinkled with fresh cilantro.

SHORBAT ADDAS
Mama's Lentil Soup

Sara Leana Ahmad
Arab and Turkoman Community
Iraq

Yield: 6 servings
Active time: 40 minutes
Total time: 1 hour

0.11 kg CO₂e This meal emits 89.49 percent less carbon than the average meal in the world's highest-emitting countries.

Sara Leana Ahmad tells stories of the Iraqi diaspora through food on her popular blog, where she shares recipes that reflect her ancestry and promote sustainability.

Ahmad believes in ethical eating and in minimizing waste, which is why she uses an entire head of celery—leaves included—to make this hearty lentil soup, a dish her mother used to cook for her. She also recommends saving the onion and lemon peels and using them to flavor broth for another soup or stew. The protein-rich red lentils fall apart and go completely soft, and the vermicelli noodles almost melt into the soup, leaving just a hint of texture. Be sure to use fine vermicelli noodles that only need to cook for a few minutes. You'll find them in Middle Eastern or Latin markets.

¼ cup (60 ml) olive oil

1 large yellow onion, halved and sliced

Salt and freshly ground black pepper

1 head celery with leaves, finely chopped

1 cup (175 g) dried red lentils

1 tablespoon ground cumin

½ tablespoon ground turmeric

¾ cup (180 ml) fresh lemon juice (from 3 lemons)

1 large bunch fresh flat-leaf parsley, leaves and thin stems only, finely chopped

½ cup (25 g) dried fine golden (toasted) vermicelli noodles

In a heavy stockpot, heat the olive oil over medium-low heat. Add the onion and cook, stirring, until browned, about 10 minutes. Using a slotted spoon or tongs, transfer the onion to a small bowl, season with salt and set aside. Place the pot over medium-high heat, add the celery and celery leaves and cook, stirring, until the celery is translucent, about 5 minutes. Season with salt and pepper. Add the red lentils, cumin and turmeric and cook, stirring, for about 2 minutes. Add 4 cups (960 ml) of water, season with salt, cover and bring to a boil. Reduce the heat and simmer, uncovered, until the lentils are soft, about 20 minutes.

Transfer the soup to a blender, place a towel on top of the lid and blend until mostly smooth with a little bit of texture.

Return the soup to the pot. Add the lemon juice, parsley and half the browned onions and stir to combine. Add the vermicelli, stir and cook on low until well combined, about 2 minutes. Ladle the soup into bowls and top with more browned onions.

VEGGIE STICK SALAD WITH DRAGON FRUIT AND STAR FRUIT

Ben Tyler
Murumburr Clan Community
Australia

Yield: 4 to 6 servings
Active time: 30 minutes
Total time: 30 minutes

0.11 kg CO₂e — This meal emits 88.54 percent less carbon than the average meal in the world's highest-emitting countries.

2 to 3 large star fruit (carambola)

1 white dragon fruit, preferably not too ripe

1 magenta dragon fruit, preferably not too ripe

2 celery stalks

1 carrot, peeled

1 red bell pepper

1 yellow bell pepper

1 small English cucumber

Fresh lemon or lime juice (optional)

"Everything we do is to raise future generations to be healthy and happy," says Ben Tyler, an indigenous chef from Kakadu in the Northern Territory of Australia. Tyler is a member of the Bininj community and part of the Murumburr clan. Inspired by his mother, grandmother, brother and ancestors, Tyler works to share Kakadu's ingredients and its legacy of sustainability.

Within the Northern Territory, non-traditional foods can be very expensive because commercial farms are far away, which increases demand and cost. Thankfully, the community is surrounded by a variety of underutilized indigenous bush foods like water lily. The entire water lily plant is edible, and it supports the local bee, goose and duck populations.

It is also the subject of a Kakadu children's book called Waterlilies *by Diane Elizabeth Lucas and Colwyn Campbell. The book follows the story of Tyler's grandmother Minnie gathering water lilies. Tyler uses water lily seed bulbs to make this fruit and vegetable salad, and he encourages you to seek them out, but also insists that this simple dish can be made with whatever produce is local and seasonal to you.*

Cut off both ends of each star fruit, then cut off the outer ridges along each star fruit. Cut lengthways to get as many long slices or sticks of fruit as possible without any seeds. Transfer to a large bowl.

Trim the ends off each dragon fruit and then cut the fruit in half. Peel off the thick skin and then cut into sticks. Add to the bowl with the star fruit.

Cut the celery, carrots, bell peppers and cucumber into thin, roughly 1 ½-inch (3.75 cm) sticks. Add to the dragon fruit and star fruit. Add the lemon or lime juice, if using, toss to combine and serve.

DANDELION SALAD TOWER WITH SORGHUM FLOUR FLATBREAD AND HONEY-CITRUS VINAIGRETTE

Ska Mirriam Moteane
Lesotho

Yield: 4 servings
Active time: 40 minutes
Total time: 40 minutes

This meal emits 87.58 percent less carbon than the average meal in the world's highest-emitting countries.

Ska Mirriam Moteane is a chef from Lesotho and the founder of the Ska Moteane Foundation, which focuses on finding sustainable solutions to food-related challenges, including providing access to healthy, local foods to underserved rural communities. Moteane is particularly passionate about promoting Basotho cuisine, which comes from an ethnic community in Southern Africa. For Moteane, food is life! She is continually inspired by the diversity of food around her and, as such, never tires of trying new things. This unique salad promotes biodiversity by incorporating dandelion, a nutritious green that grows in the wild and in the local gardens and fields around Moteane's home. It is often ignored and pulled out with nonedible weeds, but Moteane highlights its potential in this dish, along with the tomatoes, carrots, spring onion and parsley that she grows in her garden. If you are unable to find dandelion greens, you can use arugula or spinach instead.

Make the sorghum flour flatbread:

Dust a sheet pan or large platter with sorghum flour.

Peel the potato and cut into ⅛ inch-thick (0.25 cm) rounds. In a small saucepan, combine the potato slices with just enough water to cover and bring to a boil. Lower the heat and simmer until the potato is tender, about 8 minutes. Drain the potatoes, reserving the cooking water. In a small bowl, use a fork or potato masher to mash the potatoes until smooth. Gradually add about 3 tablespoons of the reserved cooking water to loosen the mash—you should have about 1 cup (250 g) of mashed potatoes.

In a medium bowl, whisk together the sorghum flour and salt. Add the mashed potatoes and use your hands to knead the flour into the potatoes. Add the cold water, as needed, 1 tablespoon at a time, to incorporate the flour and create a stiff, slightly crumbly dough. Divide the dough into 8 equal portions and roll into balls. Arrange the balls of dough on the flour-dusted sheet pan.

Lightly brush the bottom of a small nonstick pan with vegetable oil. Place a ball of dough in the center of the pan and use a spatula to press it into a thin, even round, about 5 inches (12.5 cm) in diameter—the thinner the dough, the faster it will cook. Place the pan over low heat and cook

For the sorghum flour flatbread:

1 cup (120 g) sorghum flour, plus more for dusting

1 medium (8 ounce / 225 g) potato

½ teaspoon salt

1 to 2 tablespoons cold water

Vegetable oil, for brushing the pan

For the honey-citrus vinaigrette:

¼ cup (60 ml) honey

2 tablespoons fresh lemon juice

⅛ teaspoon salt

¼ cup (60 ml) extra-virgin olive oil

1 teaspoon finely chopped fresh flat-leaf parsley leaves

For the dandelion salad:

1 bunch (about 9 ounces / 252 grams) fresh dandelion greens, tough stems removed and leaves and tender stems roughly torn

1 red bell pepper, thinly sliced

1 carrot, grated

15 cherry tomatoes, halved

2 heaping tablespoons roughly chopped spring onion

Salt and freshly ground black pepper

the flatbread until the top starts to bubble and the edges begin to brown, 1 to 2 minutes. Lightly brush the top with vegetable oil, then use a spatula to flip the flatbread and cook the other side until the edges begin to brown, 1 to 2 minutes. Remove from the heat and repeat with the remaining balls of dough, brushing the pan with oil as needed. Cut each flatbread into 4 pizza-style wedges and set aside while you make the salad.

Make the honey-citrus vinaigrette:

In a small bowl, whisk together the honey, lemon juice and salt. While whisking, slowly add the olive oil and continue whisking until fully combined. Whisk in the parsley.

Make the dandelion salad:

In a large bowl, combine the dandelion greens, bell pepper, carrot, tomatoes and spring onion. Add the dressing and toss to combine. Season with salt and pepper.

Arrange 1 flatbread wedge on a plate and top with about ¼ cup (30 g) of the salad. Continue to layer until you've used 4 flatbread wedges to create a small tower and a flatbread wedge is resting on top. Repeat with the remaining flatbread and salad and serve immediately.

WHITE BEANS WITH CHAYOTE AND SPINACH

Joan Carling
Kankanaey Community
Philippines

Yield: 4 to 6 servings
Active time: 45 minutes
Total time: 1 hour and 45 minutes, plus 8 hours soaking time

0.13 kg CO$_2$e This meal emits 87.58 percent less carbon than the average meal in the world's highest-emitting countries.

Joan Carling is an indigenous cook from Baguio City in the Philippines. Growing up steeped in Kankanaey heritage, she was taught the importance of food in nourishing our body and spirit and learned to never waste food. Food, to Carling, is an expression of her indigenous identity and culture, and used to bring people together and build resilience. Carling learned to make this comforting and nutritious bean and vegetable stew from her parents. It is both a staple dish and one that is consumed during typhoons and other emergencies because the ingredients are affordable, locally sourced and can be stored for a long period of time while still providing a well-balanced, nutritious meal. In addition to ample protein, carbohydrates, vitamins and calcium, this recipe boasts immune-supporting anti-inflammatory properties from the ginger.

2 cups (340 g) dried great Northern or cannellini beans, picked over and rinsed

3 (1-inch / 2.5 cm) pieces ginger, peeled

1 large white onion, sliced

2 fresh or dried bay leaves

Salt and freshly ground black pepper

1 chayote (mirliton), peeled and cut into cubes

½ pound (225 g) fresh spinach, stems and any thick veins removed and leaves roughly chopped

Cooked long-grain white rice, for serving

Bring 6 cups (1.4 liters) of water to a boil.

Place the beans in a large bowl. Add the just-boiled water and let stand at least 8 hours or overnight.

Drain the beans then place in a large, heavy pot. Add 4 cups (960 ml) of water, cover and bring to a boil over high heat.

Using the back of a knife, press the pieces of ginger to help release their juices, then add the ginger and any juices to the beans. Add the onion, bay leaves, 1 tablespoon salt and ½ teaspoon pepper. Reduce the heat and simmer until the beans are tender but there is still some liquid in the soup, about 45 minutes. Remove from the heat, add the chayote, cover and let steam until the chayote is cooked through but still firm, about 15 minutes. Add the spinach and cook, stirring, until the spinach wilts down and is tender, about 2 minutes. Remove and discard the bay leaves and ginger. Season with salt and pepper and serve hot with rice.

GREEN BANANA CEVICHE

Doris Goldgewicht
Costa Rica

Yield: 4 to 6 servings
Active time: 15 minutes
Total time: 1 hour

0.14 kg CO₂e — This meal emits 86.63 percent less carbon than the average meal in the world's highest-emitting countries.

4 firm, green (unripe) bananas, washed but unpeeled

¼ cup (40 g) fresh or frozen sweet corn

⅓ cup (75 ml) white wine vinegar

¼ cup (60 ml) fresh lime juice

⅓ cup (75 ml) low-sugar or no-sugar-added ketchup

½ red onion, thinly sliced

1 habanero pepper, chopped

½ red bell pepper, finely chopped

Salt and freshly ground black pepper

3 tablespoons finely chopped fresh cilantro (coriander) leaves

Baked cassava or sweet potato chips, for serving

Doris Goldgewicht is an author, teacher, chef and content creator who loves finding innovative ways to reduce food waste and support local fishmongers and farmers with her traditional Costa Rican recipes. She travels to teach culinary arts and share tips, including those that she has learned from other home cooks in her community. Goldgewicht notes that her region has fertile lands that could provide nutritious food to even its poorest citizens; however, much of its food is exported to other countries. In this plant-forward interpretation of ceviche, Goldgewicht turns to sweet and nutritious bananas, one of Costa Rica's staple crops. She leaves the peels on for cooking to reduce waste and draw out more nutrients—when boiled, banana peels provide potassium, iron and vitamins B6, C and K, as well as manganese, fiber, biotin and copper.

Bring a medium pot of water to a boil. Add the unpeeled bananas and cook until soft, about 5 minutes—the bananas and water will turn green. Remove the bananas from the water and let cool slightly. Reserve the water. Peel the bananas and cut into ¼-inch (0.5 cm) slices.

Bring the banana cooking water back to a boil. Add the corn and cook until tender, about 2 minutes. Drain and rinse under cold running water to stop the cooking.

In a large bowl, whisk together the white wine vinegar, lime juice and ketchup. Add the red onion, habanero pepper, bell pepper and corn, followed by the sliced green bananas. Gently toss to combine and season with salt and pepper. Cover and refrigerate until cold, about 2 hours.

Sprinkle with cilantro, gently toss to combine and serve with baked cassava or sweet potato chips on the side.

HAWAIIAN GREENS WITH SWEET POTATOES

Brandon Maka'awa'awa
Kanaka Maoli Community
Hawaii

Yield: 4 to 6 servings
Active time: 45 minutes
Total time: 1 hour

0.14 kg CO₂e This meal emits 86.63 percent less carbon than the average meal in the world's highest-emitting countries.

Brandon Maka'awa'awa is part of Kanaka Maoli, an indigenous community of Hawaii. He is Deputy Head of State of the Nation of Hawaii, which is the oldest Hawaiian independence organization in Hawaii, and advocates for Hawaiians to exercise and assert their national sovereignty in peaceful and meaningful ways. Maka'awa'awa works to build self-sustaining, native food environments to combat hunger, a problem that affects one in five Hawaiian children. To make this vegan, stew-like dish at home, Maka'awa'awa slowly cooks taro, a nutritious dietary staple in Hawaii, with ginger and garlic and then serves it with chunks of sweet potato. If you are unable to locate taro, you can replace it, as it was done in this recipe, with widely available spinach, which also cooks far more quickly.

In a large pot, heat the vegetable oil over medium-high heat. Add the onion, garlic and ginger, and cook until the onion is soft but not browned, 5 to 7 minutes. Season with salt. Add the vegetable broth and the spinach, stirring until wilted slightly. Bring to a boil. Reduce the heat to medium, cover and cook, stirring occasionally, until the spinach breaks down, about 15 minutes. Uncover and continue cooking until the liquid reduces, about 10 minutes. Season with salt.

Meanwhile, bring a small pot of salted water to a boil over high heat. Add the sweet potatoes, reduce the heat to medium-high and simmer until tender, 12 to 15 minutes. Drain and add to the spinach, stirring gently to combine. Season with salt and serve hot. There will likely be some liquid left in the pot. You can serve this dish with the liquid, a bit like a stew, or use a slotted spoon and scoop the veggies out.

1 tablespoon vegetable oil

½ white onion, sliced

4 garlic cloves, minced

2 (1-inch / 2.5 cm) pieces ginger, peeled and grated

Red or white Hawaiian salt

2 cups (480 ml) vegetable broth

1 pound (450 g) spinach, stems and any thick veins removed and leaves cut into strips

2 large sweet potatoes (about 250 g each), cut into 1-inch (2.5 cm) chunks

MUSHROOM "BULGOGI" SSAMBAP WITH SPICY SSAM SAUCE

Elle Youkyung Hong
South Korea

Yield: Make 4 servings
Active time: 35 minutes
Total time: 40 minutes, plus 12 hours soaking time

0.15 kg CO₂e This meal emits 85.67 percent less carbon than the average meal in the world's highest-emitting countries.

For the mushrooms:

10 dried shiitake mushrooms (about 3 ounces / 84 g)

2 tablespoons canola oil

1 medium onion, cut into thin matchsticks

1 carrot, cut into thin matchsticks

2 scallions, green parts only, chopped

1 teaspoon toasted sesame oil

2 teaspoons toasted sesame seeds

For the ssam sauce:

2 tablespoons gochujang paste

2 tablespoons apple cider vinegar

2 teaspoons sugar

1 teaspoon minced garlic

For the bulgogi sauce:

¼ cup (60 ml) soy sauce

2 tablespoons sugar

1 tablespoon minced garlic

1 tablespoon toasted sesame oil

½ teaspoon freshly ground black pepper

For the ssambap:

1 head butterhead or red leaf lettuce, leaves separated, for serving

Cooked short-grain white rice, for serving

Elle Youkyung Hong is an energetic home cook from South Korea, where "have you eaten?" is often how people say "hello," and where the popular online eating shows called Meokbang were born. Hong became passionate about the food system while studying the subject during her graduate school studies. She acknowledges issues within the food system worldwide, including food inequality, food waste, factory farming and the effects of climate change on food production, and she feels a responsibility as a food scholar to eat sustainably and share her knowledge of nutrition to combat these issues. Using dried mushrooms in this dish highlights biodiverse ingredients and also helps to combat food waste and increase nutrient content. The water from the mushrooms is used as a vegetable broth and brings earthy flavors to the soup, while popular Korean sauces bring out the natural umami flavors in the vegetables.

In a bowl, combine the dried shiitake mushrooms with enough cold water to cover. Cover and refrigerate until the insides of the mushrooms are tender and soft, at least 12 hours.

To make the ssam sauce, in a small bowl, combine the gochujang paste, apple cider vinegar, sugar and garlic and whisk until the sugar is dissolved. Cover and refrigerate at least 12 hours and up to 1 week.

To make the bulgogi sauce, in a small bowl, combine the soy sauce, sugar, garlic, sesame oil and pepper and whisk until the sugar is dissolved.

Lift the mushrooms from the soaking liquid and squeeze out any excess water. Separate the stems from the caps. Slice the caps into ¼ inch-thick (0.5 cm) slices. Cut off and discard the ends of the stems, then use your hands to tear the stems lengthwise into thin strips (or use a knife and thinly slice them). Place the mushroom caps and stems in a small bowl, add 2 tablespoons of the bulgogi sauce and toss to coat.

In a medium frying pan, heat 1 tablespoon of the canola oil over medium heat. Add the mushrooms and cook, stirring, until golden brown, 3 to 4 minutes. Remove the mushrooms from the pan and set aside.

Add the remaining 1 tablespoon of canola oil to the pan and place over medium heat. Add the onions and carrots and cook, stirring, until tender, 3 to 4 minutes. Return the mushrooms to the pan and mix well with the onions and carrots. Cook, stirring constantly, until the vegetables are fully cooked and the onions are starting to brown, 2 to 3 minutes. Add the remaining bulgogi sauce and toss to coat the vegetables. Cook, stirring, until the sauce is fully absorbed by the vegetables, 2 to 3 minutes. Add the scallion greens, mix well and remove from the heat. Add the sesame oil and toss again.

Transfer the mushroom "bulgogi" to a large plate or platter and sprinkle with the sesame seeds. Serve with the lettuce leaves, rice and ssam sauce and assemble your own ssambap.

Put a lettuce leaf in your palm and top with spoonfuls of rice and mushroom "bulgogi." Drizzle with ssam sauce, shape into a bite size ssambap pouch and enjoy.

APOTH NJUGU
Jute Mallow with Peanut Butter

Loureen Awuor
Luo Community
Kenya

Yield: 4 servings
Active time: 30 minutes
Total time: 1 hour and 15 minutes

0.16 kg CO₂e This meal emits 84.72 percent less carbon than the average meal in the world's highest-emitting countries.

Born in rural Kenya, farmer Loureen Awuor advocates for improving soil quality and planting native vegetables in East Africa, where food consumption outpaces production. As a member of the Luo indigenous community, Awuor champions seed and technology innovations to ensure that farmers and communities have access to plentiful food. Jute, which goes by many names, including jute leaf and nalta jute, is colloquially called "the king of vegetables." It is an often-overlooked relative of collard greens that can be found at all the local markets in Kenya—spinach makes a fine substitute. Awuor simmers it with creamy peanut butter and bright tomatoes for a filling dish that can be served with roasted or boiled sweet potatoes, white rice or African posho, a fluffy maize bread. If you make your own peanut butter, avoid honey-roasted peanuts, which might be too sweet, and if you only have a full-size processor, make a double batch and save the rest for another use.

Heaping ¾ cup (120 g) roasted peanuts (or ½ cup / 120 ml natural peanut butter)

4 bunches (about 800 g) jute mallow or spinach (not baby spinach)

1 teaspoon baking soda

3 tablespoons extra-virgin olive oil

1 large red onion, chopped

3 medium tomatoes, chopped

Salt

Pinch chopped fresh cayenne chili (optional)

Roasted or boiled sweet potatoes or cooked long-grain white rice, for serving

In a mini food processor, blend the peanuts on high until they break down and turn into smooth and creamy peanut butter, about 2 minutes. Measure ½ cup (120 ml) of peanut butter and set aside; reserve any extra for another use.

Pick the jute mallow leaves from the stems and chop into small pieces; discard the stems. If using spinach, cut off and discard the tough stems and chop the leaves into small pieces.

In a medium saucepan, bring 1 ½ cups (360 ml) of water to a simmer, then add the baking soda and simmer for 5 minutes. Add the jute mallow or spinach and cook, turning once, just until tender, 7 to 10 minutes for jute mallow and 2 to 3 minutes for spinach. Drain the jute mallow or spinach in a fine-mesh sieve and set aside.

In another medium saucepan, heat the olive oil over medium-high heat. Add the red onion and sauté until soft, about 3 minutes. Add the tomatoes and cook, stirring occasionally, until they release their juices and create a sauce, about 3 minutes.

Add the drained jute mallow or spinach and stir. Add the reserved ½ cup (120 ml) of peanut butter and ½ cup (120 ml) of water and stir with a wooden spoon, agitating to break up the peanut butter as needed. Simmer for 10 minutes, stirring occasionally. Season with salt and continue simmering, stirring occasionally, for 5 more minutes. Stir in the cayenne pepper, if using. Serve hot with sweet potatoes or rice.

SOUP JOUMOU

Leah Penniman
Black Kreyol Community
United States

Yield: 8 servings
Active time: 45 minutes
Total time: 1 hour and 15 minutes

0.16 kg CO₂e

This meal emits 84.72 percent less carbon than the average meal in the world's highest-emitting countries.

2 medium potatoes, chopped

2 carrots, peeled and chopped

2 leeks, chopped and well-washed

1 celery stalk, chopped

1 large onion, chopped

1 turnip, peeled and chopped

¼ white cabbage, chopped

4 garlic cloves, crushed and peeled

6 tablespoons (90 ml) olive oil

Salt and freshly ground black pepper

1 ½ pounds (675 g) kabocha squash or Caribbean pumpkin, peeled and cubed

1 (13.5 fluid ounce / 398 ml) can coconut milk

1 cup (160 g) fresh or frozen sweet corn

1 Scotch bonnet chili or other spicy chili, finely chopped

1 tablespoon chopped fresh flat-leaf parsley leaves, plus more for serving

1 tablespoon fresh lime juice

2 whole cloves

1 teaspoon dried thyme

1 tablespoon honey or sweetener of your choice (optional)

Leah Penniman is a Black Kreyol farmer/peyizan, author and food justice activist. She co-founded Soul Fire Farm with the mission to end racism in the food system and reclaim ancestral connection to the land through Afro-indigenous farming practices, farming training for Black and Brown people, a subsidized farm food distribution program and widespread organizing toward equity in the food system. Penniman's farm grows 100 percent of the ingredients used in this heritage recipe for Soup Joumou, "the soup of independence," that is made every new year to celebrate Haiti's liberation from France.

Preheat the oven to 400°F (200°C).

On a sheet pan, toss the potatoes, carrots, leeks, celery, onion, turnip, cabbage and garlic with 4 tablespoons (60 ml) of the olive oil. Season with salt and pepper and roast, stirring occasionally, until golden and tender, about 40 minutes.

Meanwhile, on a second sheet pan, toss the squash with the remaining 2 tablespoons of olive oil. Season with salt and pepper and roast, stirring occasionally, until golden brown and tender, about 30 minutes.

In a blender or food processor, combine the roasted squash and coconut milk and blend until mostly smooth. Transfer to a large pot, add 8 cups (1.9 liters) of water and bring to a low boil. Add the roasted vegetables, along with the corn, Scotch bonnet chili, parsley, lime juice, cloves and thyme. Season with salt and pepper and add the honey, if using. Continue to gently boil for 15 to 20 minutes to blend the flavors.

Divide among bowls, sprinkle with parsley and serve.

Rosalia Chay Chuc
Mayan Community
Mexico

Niyati Parekh
India

Sean Sherman
Oglala Lakota Community
United States

Manal Al Alem
Jordan

Rina Matsuo
Ryukyu Community
Japan

Gloria and Juana Hidalgo
Dominican Republic

Sara Leana Ahmad
Arab and Turkoman Community
Iraq

Ben Tyler
Murumburr Clan Community
Australia

Ska Mirriam Moteane
Lesotho

Joan Carling
Kankanaey Community
Philippines

Doris Goldgewicht
Costa Rica

Brandon Maka'awa'awa
Kanaka Maoli Community
Hawaii

Elle Youkyung Hong
South Korea

Loureen Awuor
Luo Community
Kenya

Leah Penniman
Black Kreyol Community
United States

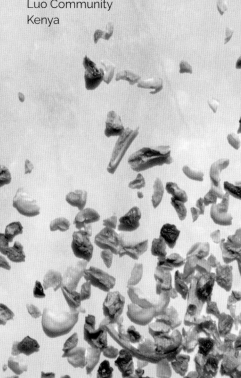

V. Reducing Food Waste

Rediscovering the Value of Food

Food connects us all. We all need it, depend on it,
survive thanks to it and derive happiness from it.

We all love food. Food fulfills our cravings and delights our palates. Food is part of our collective identity, our habits and our cultures. We treasure recipes that remind us of special people and places. We gather around holiday tables, countertops and street corners to break bread and build community. The sight, smell and experience of food is all around us. And yet, we often take food for granted and waste it.

Before sitting down to eat, how many of us stop to think about where our food comes from or how much labor is required to move food from plot to plate? When we do, we are more conscientious about how much of this precious resource gets lost in the process.

Great effort and cost are required to grow, harvest, process, package, transport and distribute food to consumers in the convenient forms we have come to know and expect.

The amount of food that is lost from its harvest, up to but not including the retail level, is referred to as *food loss*. The amount wasted at the consumer and retail level is referred to as *food waste*. We make this distinction to demonstrate that this is a ubiquitous problem and emphasize that everyone—from farmers and producers to consumers and shop owners—can help eliminate it.

Food loss and waste are systemic problems, meaning that they occur at every step of the food supply chain. From production to consumption—in packaging plants, supermarkets, restaurants and homes—valuable food is not reaching its destination. Industrialized countries in particular waste large quantities of edible food at the consumer level by over-buying, over-ordering and incorrectly storing food.

The consumer-facing system does not help: Many of us are confused by "best-before" (the date until when the food retains its expected quality) and "use-by" (the date until when the food can be eaten safely) indicators on food packages and, out of caution, throw away food that is perfectly fit for consumption. To clarify: Food is still safe to consume after the indicated best-before date, provided that the item's storage instructions are respected and its packaging is not damaged. We should rely on our (common) senses instead!

Supermarkets are another area of immense loss. Large quantities of fruits and vegetables are discarded because they do not conform to the public's perception of "good quality." Produce that is small or misshapen—so-called "ugly fruits"—is often passed over and left to spoil when it still carries as much flavor and nutrition as its picture-perfect counterparts.

As all of this food is wasted, 700 to 900 million people on our planet are estimated to be hungry at any given time, and 3 billion (almost half of the world's population) cannot afford a healthy diet. This is unacceptable and warrants urgent attention and action.

Food waste has untenable environmental impacts as well. Food that is produced but ultimately wasted still requires large quantities of increasingly scarce natural resources to grow. This includes land, water, agricultural inputs, energy, harvest and processing labor, and transportation operations. Further, when food makes its way to landfills, it decomposes anaerobically, creating methane, a greenhouse gas twenty times as harmful to the atmosphere as carbon dioxide.

The large quantity of food sitting in landfills instead of on tables contributes to both hunger and global warming. This makes reducing food waste an inarguable way to address the interconnected sustainability challenges of climate change, food security and natural resource shortages. Minimizing food waste offers us a way to increase food security, while strengthening economic and social development and promoting sustainability.

INNOVATIVE SOLUTIONS TO FOOD WASTE

Technological innovation has played a vital role in tackling food waste worldwide and will continue to be a key player in our fight for sustainability. Countless mobile apps and online systems are connecting consumers to rapid food distribution platforms, while being mindful of waste and carbon footprint. Grocery stores and farms that struggle with unsold items are increasingly turning to these new technologies to facilitate the sale of unsold food that is fit to eat, and we should continue to explore new pathways that compensate producers fairly while helping food reach hungry mouths. Enhanced organic produce packaging and farmer-to-consumer weekly deliveries are just the tip of the iceberg; by working together across sectors and agendas, we can develop additional ways to waste less and do more—for ourselves and generations to come.

RECOVERY AND REDISTRIBUTION (R&R)
OF SAFE AND NUTRITIOUS FOOD

In our efforts to minimize food waste, we may find that large amounts of food can be "rescued" from the bin. Food recovery and redistribution refers to first saving food from being wasted and then redistributing it to families and communities in need. In both developed countries where people are combating micronutrient deficiencies and developing nations that are battling hunger, these services provide a literal lifeline for those in need.

As individuals, we can use our time and dollars to support recovery and redistribution services that offer discounted or free nutritious food to those with limited resources—and demand that our community and national leaders do the same.

Many of our communities have R&R services that exist in different formats, including food banks, soup kitchens and social supermarkets. In some cases, prepackaged food boxes are distributed to recipients, and in others, the beneficiary has more freedom in the selection process. Both help connect our neighbors to nutrients. Ensuring that food-insecure individuals get both enough food *and* enough nutrients makes these programs successful on two fronts.

ACTIONS WE CAN TAKE TODAY

Some easy actions we can all take to reduce food waste for healthier communities and a healthier planet include:

1. BUY ONLY WHAT WE NEED.

By planning our meals, making a shopping list, sticking to it and limiting impulse buys, we can waste less food while saving money and time.

2. PICK UGLY FRUIT AND VEGETABLES.

In the same way that we should not judge a book by its cover, we should not judge a fruit by its shape. We often throw away oddly shaped or bruised fruits and vegetables, because they do not meet arbitrary cosmetic standards. But worry not—they taste the same! If fruit is over-ripe, we can still purchase it to freeze for making smoothies, juices and desserts.

3. STORE FOOD WISELY.

Shifting older products to the front of our cupboards and refrigerators and newer items to the back helps us use our purchases in a timely manner. Using airtight containers and re-usable, sealed bags can ensure that products stay fresh and protected from insects or other disturbances.

4. UNDERSTAND FOOD LABELLING.

Remember the difference between "best-before" and "use-by" dates. Often, a food is still safe to eat after the "best-before" date, whereas the "use-by" date serves as a hard stop.

5. START SMALL.

Sharing large dishes "family style" at restaurants and being mindful of our portions at home helps ensure that less food is wasted from overserving.

6. LOVE OUR LEFTOVERS.

The freezer is our friend! Using leftovers as ingredients in another meal, or freezing them to enjoy later, is a great way to reduce time spent in the kitchen, as well as food in the bin.

7. USE WASTE WISELY.

Another way to give leftovers new life is by composting them, which returns nutrients to the soil and reduces our carbon footprint at the same time.

8. RESPECT FOOD.

Food connects us all. Educating ourselves about the food system, getting to know our farmers and asking questions about how food gets from soil to supermarket is a way to return to a respectful relationship with the seeds, land and people that nourish us.

9. FIND NEW WAYS TO SHARE.

Using new technologies or innovations, we can rally a network of community members and local businesses that share surplus food rather than discarding it.

These actions impact our immediate communities, and if communities everywhere employ them more broadly, they have the power to positively change our global food system.

COCONUT AND TOMATO STEW

Julius Roberts
England

Yield: Makes 4 to 6 servings
Active time: 15 minutes
Total time: 35 minutes

Julius Roberts is a self-taught, first-generation farmer who traded his restaurant career for a more sustainability-focused life in the English countryside. After leaving London and starting his small farm with just four pigs, he began using social media—and his professional kitchen skills—to encourage others to minimize food waste, garden at home and commit to supporting local purveyors. In this simple yet bursting-with-flavor recipe, Roberts uses end-of-season tomatoes that are full and juicy, along with warming spices and coconut milk, for a satisfying, wholesome dish that can be served alone or with basmati rice for a more substantial meal.

Preheat the oven to 450°F (230°C).

In a 9 x 13-inch (23 x 33 cm) or similar-sized baking dish, toss the tomatoes with 2 tablespoons of the olive oil and season with salt. Roast until soft and wilted, 15 to 20 minutes.

Meanwhile, in a large pot, heat the remaining 2 tablespoons of olive oil over medium-high heat. Add the onion, garlic, chilis, lemongrass and ginger and cook, stirring, until the onion is soft but not browned, 7 to 10 minutes. Add the lime leaves, star anise, allspice berries, cardamom and ground allspice and cook, stirring, until fragrant, about 2 minutes. Add the coconut milk and turmeric. Add about ½ cup (120 ml) of water to one of the empty coconut milk cans, swish it around, and add the liquid to the pot. Stir and bring to a simmer, using a wooden spoon to scrape any bits off the bottom of the pot. Continue simmering, stirring occasionally, until the curry has thickened, 15 to 20 minutes. Remove from the heat.

Using a slotted spoon, remove and discard the lemongrass, lime leaves, star anise and allspice berries. Stir in the ¼ cup (70 g) of yogurt. Using a slotted spoon, scoop the roasted tomatoes into the pot, leaving the juices behind—save them to flavor soup or stew. Stir to heat the tomatoes then divide among bowls. Top with a dollop of yogurt, sprinkle with cilantro and serve.

3 pounds (1.3 kg) cocktail or other small tomatoes, preferably in multiple colors

4 tablespoons (60 ml) olive oil

Salt

1 large yellow onion, thinly sliced

3 garlic cloves, finely chopped

2 fresh red or green chilis, thinly sliced

1 lemongrass stalk, tough outer leaves, bulb and upper stalk discarded and remaining stalk bruised with the back of a knife

1 (2-inch / 5 cm) piece ginger, peeled and grated

3 fresh or frozen makrut lime leaves

4 whole star anise

4 whole allspice berries

1 tablespoon ground cardamom

2 teaspoons ground allspice

1 (13.5-fluid ounce / 398 ml) can coconut milk

2 tablespoons ground turmeric

¼ cup (70 g) Greek yogurt, plus more for serving

Fresh cilantro (coriander) leaves, for serving

NONNA ANCELLA'S PASSATELLI

Massimo Bottura
Italy

Yield: 4 servings
Active time: 20 minutes
Total time: 1 hour and 30 minutes

¾ cup (100 g) fine dry breadcrumbs, from a crusty loaf containing only flour, yeast, water and salt*

¾ cup (50 g) finely grated Parmigiano-Reggiano cheese, plus more for serving

¼ teaspoon finely grated lemon zest

⅛ teaspoon freshly ground nutmeg

3 sustainably sourced large eggs, lightly beaten

6 cups (1.4 liters) chicken broth, preferably homemade

Massimo Bottura is a chef and food activist from Moderna, Italy. Alongside his wife, Lara Gilmore, he founded Food for Soul, a non-profit organization dedicated to caring for "people, places and food" by combating food waste and food insecurity throughout Italy and around the world. Massimo learned this passatelli recipe from his nonna (grandmother) and continues to pass it down in his family today. Humble breadcrumbs transform into flavorful pasta, which is served in a warming broth for a dish that reduces waste while being playful and satisfying.

Combine the breadcrumbs, Parmigiano-Reggiano, lemon zest and nutmeg in a bowl. Add the eggs and stir to combine well. Using your hands, form the dough into a disk. Set the dough in the bowl, cover the bowl with plastic wrap and let stand at room temperature for 1 hour.

In a large pot, bring the chicken broth to a boil. Reduce the heat and simmer.

After the dough has rested and while the chicken broth is simmering, line a large sheet pan with parchment paper.

Cut the dough into quarters. Working with a quarter of the dough at a time, push the dough through a food/meat grinder with large (¼-inch / 0.5 cm) holes and cut with a sharp knife into 3-inch (7.5 cm) pieces (Alternatively, use a passatelli maker or a potato ricer with large holes.) Place the passatelli on the prepared sheet pan, being careful that the pieces do not touch. Repeat with the remaining dough. Let the passatelli dry slightly, about 10 minutes.

Working in two batches, gently drop the passatelli into the simmering broth and cook, gently stirring, until they rise to the surface, about 1 minute. With a slotted spoon, divide the passatelli among four warm bowls. Spoon the hot broth over the passatelli, sprinkle with Parmigiano-Reggiano and serve.

*Using bread made with only flour, yeast, water and salt is essential to this recipe's success. If your bread is not dry, bake slices in a 350°F (180°C) oven for 15 to 20 minutes or until dry. Let cool and then process in a food processor fit with a metal blade until fine.

MUSHROOM BOUREK

Saliha Bala
Kabylic community
Algeria

Yield: 10 to 12 boureks
Active time: 60 minutes
Total time: 1 hour and 30 minutes

Saliha Bala is a French-Algerian home cook who lives in Champigny-sur-Marne, France. She supports a more sustainable and minimalistic way of life to improve planetary health and provide a better future for her son. With millions of people around the world dying from hunger and complications due to malnutrition, Bala feels that the food system is fundamentally inequitable, and she wants to be a part of the change to make it more just. Her mushroom-filled boureks are both tasty and comforting. They can also be baked for 15 to 20 minutes in a 400°F (200°C) oven until golden and crispy. To reduce waste, boureks can be filled with traditional vegetables or sustainably sourced meats that might be in your fridge. Bala would normally use warka, another type of thin pastry, but this recipe uses phyllo as it is widely available and makes a great substitute.

2 cups plus 3 tablespoons (525 ml) sunflower oil, plus more for sealing the boureks

1 medium yellow onion, finely chopped

1 carrot, finely chopped

2 tablespoons finely chopped celery

2 garlic cloves, minced

1 (1-inch / 2.5 cm) piece ginger, peeled and grated

20 ounces (560 g) cremini mushrooms, sliced

1 teaspoon smoked paprika

1 teaspoon ground cumin

1 teaspoon ground caraway

1 teaspoon salt

½ teaspoon freshly ground black pepper

1 tablespoon tomato paste

1 tablespoon nutritional yeast

¼ cup (13 g) finely chopped fresh flat-leaf parsley leaves

12 sheets phyllo dough, thawed overnight if frozen

Finely chopped fresh chives, for serving

In a large deep skillet, heat 3 tablespoons of the sunflower oil over medium heat. Add the onion, carrot, celery, garlic and ginger and cook, stirring often, until tender, about 5 minutes. If the pan gets too dry, add a small splash of water to keep the vegetables from burning. Add the mushrooms and cook, stirring often, until they release their liquid and then the liquid evaporates, 8 to 10 minutes. Stir in the paprika, cumin, caraway, salt and pepper and cook, stirring, about 30 seconds. Add the tomato paste, stir well to mix with the mushrooms and cook, stirring, for 1 minute. Transfer to a medium bowl, add the nutritional yeast and parsley and let cool.

Carefully unroll the defrosted phyllo sheets, cover with plastic wrap or wax paper, followed by a damp towel.

Set one piece of phyllo in front of you with a long side facing you. Use a knife, scissors or pizza cutter to cut 3 inches (7.5 cm) off one of the shorter sides. Discard the scraps or reserve for another use. Place a roughly golf ball–sized ball of the mushroom mixture about 1 inch (2.5 cm) from the edge closest to you. Shape the mushroom mixture into a roughly 5-inch-long (12.5 cm) sausage shape, leaving about 1 inch (2.5 cm) between the dough and the edge of the phyllo.

Carefully fold the long side closest to you up and over the mushroom mixture. Fold both short sides up and over the mushroom mixture—the sides should overlap. Gently roll the pastry away from you and around the filling to create a loose cigar shape. Lightly brush the inside edge with sunflower oil and press lightly to seal.

Repeat to make the remaining boureks and arrange, with their seams facing down, in a single layer on a platter or sheet pan. Cover loosely with a towel.

Line a sheet pan with paper towels and set near the stove.

Fill the same large, deep skillet used to cook the mushrooms with enough of the remaining sunflower oil to come about 1 inch (2.5 cm) up the sides. Place over medium-high heat and bring to 325°F (163°C) on a deep-fry thermometer. Working in batches, carefully add the boureks to the oil and fry, turning once, until browned on both sides, 2 to 3 minutes total. Transfer to the paper towel-lined sheet pan to drain. Sprinkle with chives and serve hot.

ERDÄPFELGULASCH
Austrian-Style Potato Goulash

Ursula Schersch
Austria

Yield: 4 to 6 servings
Active time: 35 minutes
Total time: 1 hour

3 tablespoons vegetable oil

2 medium yellow onions, diced

2 garlic cloves, minced

2 tablespoons tomato paste

2 tablespoons Hungarian paprika (or other mild paprika)

½ teaspoon caraway seeds

½ teaspoon dried marjoram (optional)

½ tablespoon sherry vinegar

5 cups (1.2 liters) hot vegetable broth

2 fresh or dried bay leaves

Salt and freshly ground black pepper

2 pounds (900 g) starchy potatoes, such as russet or Yukon gold, unpeeled and cut into 1-inch (2.5 cm) cubes

Chopped fresh flat-leaf parsley leaves, vegan crème fraîche and bread, for serving

Ursula Schersch is a cookbook author, food journalist and food photographer based in Vienna, Austria. She writes food blogs in both English and German and uses them to promote cooking with seasonal, local ingredients and fermented foods. Schersch's take on goulash reveals the influence of growing up on a small farm with a sustainable approach to living where reducing food waste was standard. She does not peel the potatoes—as the skins add extra nutrients—and often adds vegetable odds and ends for additional fiber and color. Schersch also has a clever, vegan-friendly trick for thickening the soup: Instead of adding cream, she mashes some of the potatoes and stirs them back in for extra richness.

In a large pot, heat the vegetable oil over medium-high heat. Add the onions and cook, stirring often, until soft and golden, about 10 minutes. Add the garlic and cook, stirring often, for 1 minute. Add the tomato paste, paprika, caraway seeds and marjoram, if using, and stir for about 10 seconds. Add the vinegar and deglaze the pan, using a wooden spoon to scrape any bits off the bottom. Immediately add the hot vegetable broth, bay leaves, ¼ teaspoon salt and a few grinds of black pepper and bring to a boil. Add the potatoes, stir, cover and gently boil until the potatoes are tender, 20 to 25 minutes.

Transfer a generous handful of the potatoes and a few tablespoons of the sauce to a small bowl. Use a fork to mash the mixture together and then return it to the pot, stir and cook over medium-low heat until the goulash thickens, about 15 minutes.

Season with salt and pepper.

Divide the goulash among bowls and sprinkle with parsley. Top with a dollop of vegan crème fraîche and serve with bread.

CARROT BIRYANI

Niven Patel
India

Yield: 6 servings
Active time: 45 minutes
Total time: 1 hour and 15 minutes

Chef Niven Patel worked throughout the Cayman Islands and Europe before opening a restaurant and two-acre farm that serves his local Miami community. Despite living in an urban environment, Patel strives to grow his own food and raise awareness about the amount of labor that goes into every dish he serves. When he makes this carrot biryani, he uses homegrown carrots and saves the tops for compost. Flavored with Indian herbs and spices, this dish is both hearty and delicate and makes a perfect partner to your favorite dal.

Make the rice:

Gently rinse the rice under running water, then drain and place in a large pot. Add 4 cups (960 ml) of water, the vegetable oil, salt, cinnamon sticks, bay leaves, cloves, cardamom pods and garam masala and bring to a boil. Reduce the heat to medium-low and cook until the rice is al dente, 3 to 5 minutes—there will still be a lot of water left in the saucepan. Do not over-cook the rice. It will cook again with the vegetables so should only be 50 to 70 percent done at this point. Remove from the heat and drain the excess water.

Soak the saffron in the warm milk for a few minutes then fold it into the rice. Set aside.

Make the vegetables:

Preheat the oven to 350°F (180°C).

Beat the yogurt until smooth and creamy. Set aside.

Heat the oil or ghee in a pan over medium-high heat. Test the heat by adding 1 cumin seed to the oil; if the seed cracks right away, it is ready. Add the remaining cumin seeds and cook until they crack, about 1 minute. Add the turmeric and onion and cook, stirring, until the onion is soft, about 2 minutes. Add the ginger and garlic and cook, stirring, for 1 minute. Add the potato and carrots and cook, stirring occasionally and covering when not stirring, about 5 minutes. When vegetables begin to catch, sizzling against the bottom of the pan, stir in the tomatoes and cook until the carrots and potato are tender, about 6 more minutes. Add the green beans, serrano chili, garam masala and red chili powder, stirring to combine. Season with salt. Remove from the heat and allow to cool slightly. Gradually stir in the yogurt, a few tablespoons at a time. The yogurt might curdle a little, but this is fine.

Spread half the vegetable mixture in a deep 9 x 13 inch (23 x 33 cm) or similar-sized baking dish. Top with half of the rice mixture, spreading it evenly to cover the vegetables. Sprinkle with the mint and cilantro, then top with the remaining vegetable mixture, spreading it evenly. Top with the re-maining rice mixture, spreading it evenly. Spread the melted butter over the entire surface. Cover with foil and bake until starting to bubble in the cor-ners, about 30 minutes. Let stand for a few minutes, then sprinkle with more mint and cilantro and serve.

For the rice:
1 cup (200g) basmati rice
1 tablespoon vegetable oil
½ teaspoon salt
2 cinnamon sticks
2 bay leaves
2 whole cloves
2 green cardamom pods
Pinch of garam masala
2 pinches saffron threads
1 tablespoon warm whole milk

For the vegetables:
½ cup to 1 cup (113 to 226 g) full- or low-fat plain yogurt
2 tablespoons vegetable oil or ghee
1 teaspoon cumin seed
½ teaspoon ground turmeric
½ large white onion, chopped
1 teaspoon freshly grated ginger
1 large garlic clove, minced
1 large yellow potato, such as Yukon gold, cut into cubes
6 medium carrots, sliced
4 medium tomatoes, chopped
Handful of green beans, trimmed and chopped
1 serrano chili, finely chopped
½ teaspoon garam masala
½ teaspoon red chili powder
Salt
¼ cup (10 g) chopped fresh mint and cilantro (coriander) leaves, plus more for serving
1 tablespoon unsalted butter or ghee, melted

SAMLOR KORKO
Cambodian Stirring Pot Soup

Sotha Sok
Cambodia

Yield: 6 to 8 servings
Active time: 30 minutes
Total time: 60 minutes

2 tablespoons vegetable oil

¼ cup (50 g) green kroeung

2 (6-ounce / 170 g) sustainably sourced skinless catfish, tilapia or other mild fish fillets

2 tablespoons roasted ground rice

2 tablespoons fish sauce

1 tablespoon prahok

2 tablespoons palm or brown sugar

2 tablespoons salt

7 ounces (200 g) Chinese eggplant, cut into bite-size pieces

7 ounces (200 g) butternut squash, peeled, seeds removed and cut into small pieces

20 green beans, trimmed and cut into small pieces

7 ounces (200 g) green papaya, peeled and cut into small pieces

7 ounces (200 g) green (unripe) jackfruit, peeled and cut into small pieces

2 green bananas, peeled and cut into small pieces

Sotha Sok is a Cambodian farmer from Svay Rieng, where he is an ally for climate-resistant local agriculture. This traditional Khmer recipe requires less cooking water than similar dishes, instead utilizing the natural moisture from vegetables that Sok sources from local smallholder farmers. Alongside green beans, green papaya, jackfruit and green banana, this one-pot dish lets no product go to waste and showcases signature Cambodian ingredients like green kroeung, a lemongrass paste made with galangal and turmeric, and prahok, a fermented fish paste. If you cannot find fermented fish paste, use additional fish sauce. Roasted ground rice, which may be labeled toasted ground rice, helps to thicken the soup.

In a large stockpot, heat the vegetable oil over medium-high heat. Add the green kroeung and fish and fry, turning the fish as needed, until aromatic, 3 to 4 minutes. Add the roasted ground rice, fish sauce, prahok, palm or brown sugar and salt and stir to combine. Add the eggplant, butternut squash, green beans, green papaya, jackfruit and green banana. Add 5 cups (1.2 liters) of water, gently stir, and bring to a simmer. Continue simmering, uncovered and stirring occasionally, until the vegetables are tender, approximately 30 minutes. Serve hot.

CHARRED CABBAGE

Adrian Hădean
Romania

Yield: 6 servings
Active time: 10 minutes
Total time: 1 hour and 20 minutes

Adrian Hădean is a Romanian chef who has dedicated his life to traveling the world and exploring the endless ways food can be prepared and enjoyed. He is fascinated by the billions of dishes he has yet to cook and seemingly endless ingredients still unfamiliar to him. He is inspired to learn as many of those dishes as he can in his lifetime. This earthy and unexpected dish honors Hădean's Romanian heritage by using locally sourced ingredients and is high in dietary fiber and vitamins C and K. The black truffle adds a bit of indulgence to an otherwise rustic dish but is completely optional—the cabbage is still dynamite without it. This recipe offers a great way to reduce food waste, should you have limited ingredients but want to create a wonderful dish. Save the parsley and dill strained out of the oil, seasoned with salt and pepper, as they make a fantastic rub for meat or a spread for toast.

1 medium white cabbage (about 2 pounds / 900 g)

3 tablespoons chopped fresh flat-leaf parsley

1 tablespoon chopped fresh dill

½ cup (120 ml) extra-virgin olive oil

Salt and fresh ground black pepper

2 to 3 tablespoons red or white wine vinegar

1 (8-ounce / 225 g) container crème fraîche or really rich sour cream

Black truffle, sliced (optional)

Preheat the oven to 500°F (260°C).

Place the cabbage on a sheet pan and roast until black all over, about 1 hour, or longer if the cabbage is particularly dense.

Meanwhile, in a blender or food processor, combine the parsley and dill. With the blender on low, slowly add the olive oil in a thin stream. Once all the oil is added, blend on high for 1 minute more. Season with salt and pepper. Strain the oil and set aside.

When the cabbage is black, lightly hit it with a fork to loosen the outer blackened layer; discard those layers. Let the cabbage stand briefly until cool enough to handle. Cut the cabbage into slices, discarding any tough core. Arrange on a platter, drizzle with the vinegar to taste and season with salt and pepper. Top with dollops of crème fraîche or sour cream, drizzle with the herb oil and sprinkle with black truffle slices, if using. Serve hot or at room temperature.

PICCALILLI

Eelke Plasmeijer
The Netherlands

Yield: 5 (8-ounce / 240 ml) jars
Active time: 1 hour
Total time: 1 hour, plus 24 hours for salting and 4 to 6 weeks for maturing

2 ¼ pounds (1 kg) mixed vegetables, such as: cauliflower, green beans, cucumber, green tomatoes or shallots

2 ½ tablespoons sea salt

½ cup (60 g) cornstarch

2 ½ tablespoons ground turmeric

2 ½ tablespoons mustard powder

3 tablespoons yellow mustard seeds

2 teaspoons cumin seeds, crushed

2 teaspoons coriander seeds, crushed

2 ½ cups (600 ml) white wine vinegar

¾ cup plus two tablespoons (175 g) sugar

½ cup (120 ml) honey

Eelke Plasmeijer is a Dutch chef and restaurateur living in Ubud, Bali, Indonesia. His dreams of becoming a cook were awakened during childhood when he baked bread with his grandfather for the first time and, for the next few days, wanted to eat only that bread. After moving to Indonesia, Plasmeijer's view of cooking was transformed by the local culinary culture, which ignited his desire to inspire others to celebrate their healthful traditions and combat the omnipresence of Western ideals. Indonesia grapples with the consequences of being a quickly developing country. With all the good that economic growth brings, it is also attributed to the increased consumption of ultra-processed foods, sugar-sweetened beverages and meat. Plasmeijer suggests each country look inward before trying to fix others. In his restaurant, he honors and supports the community in which he lives by sourcing ingredients from local farmers. While this simple pickle is a recipe Plasmeijer used to make with his Belgian aunt, it can be customized with in-season vegetables local to your area and salvage those that might otherwise be wasted. Plasmeijer recommends serving it alongside a hearty stew or as part of a cheese plate.

To sterilize jars, wash and dry 5 (8-ounce / 240 ml) jars thoroughly. Place the jars and jar lids in a large stockpot filled with water. Bring to a boil and continue boiling for 5 minutes. Keep the jars and jar lids in the hot water until ready to use.

Cut the vegetables into even, pea-sized pieces. Place into a large bowl and sprinkle with the salt. Mix well, cover with a towel and let stand in a cool place for 24 hours.

Rinse the vegetables with ice cold water and drain thoroughly. Pat dry as needed so the vegetables are as dry as possible.

In a small bowl, whisk together the cornstarch, turmeric, mustard powder, mustard seeds, cumin and coriander. Add ½ cup to ¾ cup (120 to 180 ml) vinegar to create a paste and whisk until smooth.

In a medium saucepan, combine the remaining vinegar with the sugar and honey and bring to a boil. Add the cornstarch-spice mixture and return to a boil, whisking constantly. Continue boiling until thick, 3 to 4 minutes. Remove from the heat and carefully fold the well-dried vegetables into the hot, spicy sauce.

Remove the sterilized jars from the hot water and place them on a clean, dry kitchen towel. Reserve the pot of hot water. Sterilize a ladle by submerging it in the hot water for a few seconds. Carefully ladle the hot piccalilli into the warm sterilized jars and fill them up to ½ inch (1.25 cm) below the rim. Using a wooden spoon, poke along the inside of the jars, making sure you remove any air pockets. Wipe the lip of the jars with a clean, damp kitchen towel to ensure a proper seal, then top with the lids and seal.

Carefully lift the filled and sealed jars and place them back in the original pot of hot water, making sure there are at least a couple inches of water covering the jars. Depending on the number of jars and the size of the pot, you may need to tuck kitchen towels in and around them to prevent them from rattling. Bring to a boil and continue boiling for 10 minutes.

Carefully remove the hot jars from the pot and place on a clean, dry kitchen towel. Let sit, undisturbed, overnight at room temperature to ensure a proper seal. Let the piccalilli mature in a cool, dark place for 4 to 6 weeks.

SHAMDEY

Jamsel Gyaltshen
Bhutan

Yields: 4 servings
Active time: 25 minutes
Total time: 35 minutes

Jamsel Gyaltshen is a young Bhutanese chef and restaurant owner from the capital city of Thimphu. After training at the Culinary Institute of America, he returned to explore what he describes as the "untapped potential" of Bhutanese ingredients while integrating new techniques in traditional dishes. This fragrant dish from Gyaltshen's mother's side of the family is typically served at special gatherings or on ceremonial occasions. It is a quick, plant-forward dish, offering an opportunity to utilize odds and ends, and highlights overlooked ingredients.

Fill a medium bowl with ice water.

Bring a small pot of salted water to a boil. Carefully add the eggs and cook for 12 minutes. Use a slotted spoon to transfer the eggs to the ice water and let cool completely. Once the eggs are cool, peel and set aside.

In a wok or large frying pan, melt the butter over medium-high heat. Add the ginger and cook, stirring, until fragrant and soft, about 2 minutes. Add the cooked rice, stir to coat and season with salt. Continue cooking the rice, stirring constantly, until crispy and sticking to the pan, about 7 minutes. Add the chilis and cook, stirring constantly, until fragrant, about 3 minutes. Remove from the heat, stir in the cilantro and season with salt. Crumble the hard-boiled eggs on top, garnish with more cilantro and serve.

4 large eggs

6 tablespoons (84 g) unsalted butter

1 (6-inch / 15 cm) piece ginger, peeled and grated

4 cups (1 kg) cooked rice

Salt

1 cup (125 g) finely chopped fresh Thai, jalapeño or other green chilis

½ cup (21 g) finely chopped fresh cilantro (coriander) leaves, plus whole leaves for serving

JOSEPHINE'S QUICHE LORRAINE

Lisa Johnson
Antarctica

Yield: 6 to 8 servings
Active time: 15 minutes, plus more time if making a homemade pastry shell
Total time: 1 hour and 15 minutes

1 (9-inch / 23-cm) homemade or premade pastry shell

1 tablespoon unsalted butter

⅓ cup (60 g) diced yellow onion

3 sustainably sourced large eggs, beaten

1 ¼ cups (300 ml) heavy cream or half-and-half

⅛ teaspoon freshly grated nutmeg

¾ teaspoon salt

½ teaspoon freshly ground black pepper

1 cup (135 g) cooked ham, cut into ½-inch (1.25 cm) pieces, or high-quality deli ham, preferably thick-cut, chopped

1 ¼ cups (135 g) shredded Gruyère

When working in Antarctica where she cooked homestyle meals for NASA scientists, chef Lisa Johnson's primary mission was to keep her crews' spirits up while simultaneously ensuring that their unique nutritional needs were being met. With 35 years of experience in the field, Lisa has seen many changes in our food supplies: industrial agricultural practices of using large scale mono-crop production are more common, our seas are being overfished at an alarming rate and we are not allowing our ecosystem to recover so that it can continue to meet our long-term needs. Johnson hopes that we can all do our part to make our food system better for future generations by buying locally from farmers and distributors that focus on sustainability and total utilization, and by making each meal with a "HUGE dollop of love," just like her mother used to do.

Cooking in Antarctica comes with a unique set of exciting challenges, as it is very difficult to transport food to such an isolated region. As such, daily meals are carefully planned to minimize waste and in accordance with what is available. For this recipe, Johnson cooked the quiches in the central galley and then transported them out to the camp. She gently reheated the cooked quiches in the oven instead of preparing them onsite because chefs were not allowed to have raw eggs at the camp, for fear of introducing the bird flu to their somewhat frequent Adeile penguin visitors. Johnson credits her mother for the inspiration behind this quiche, as well as her ability to be flexible in the kitchen—it can be made with different ingredients and is a great way to use leftovers from the fridge, cutting back on food waste. It is also satiating and nutritious, giving scientists a "little oasis on the ice."

Set a rack in the middle of the oven and preheat the oven to 375°F (190°C).

Set the pastry shell on a sheet pan. Poke the pastry shell all over with a fork, then line with foil and fill with pie weights or dried beans. Bake for 15 minutes before removing the pie weights and foil, and conitnue baking until golden, 10 more minutes. Set the baked pastry shell on a rack while you make the filling. Leave the oven on.

In a small frying pan, melt the butter over medium heat. Add the onion and cook, stirring, until soft and lightly browned, 6 to 8 minutes. Remove from the heat and set aside.

In a large bowl, whisk together the eggs, heavy cream, nutmeg, salt and pepper.

Sprinkle the onion, ham and shredded cheese in the bottom of the prebaked pastry shell. Pull the center rack out of the oven and place the sheet pan and filled pastry shell on the rack. Carefully pour the egg mixture into the pastry shell and then gently push the rack back into place. Bake for 15 minutes, then reduce the oven temperature to 325°F (163°C) and bake until the quiche no longer jiggles when lightly shaken, about 30 minutes.

Let cool on a rack for about 20 minutes, then slice and serve.

MAKE DO RATATOU(ILLE)

Danielle Nierenberg
United States

Yield: 6 servings
Active time: 40 minutes
Total time: 3 hours and 10 minutes

Danielle Neirenberg is an activist, author, journalist and President of Food Tank, a think tank and research organization dedicated to building a global community for safe, healthy, nourished eaters. In addition to on-the-ground research, Food Tank presents annual summits that bring together representatives from across the food system, including those from universities and food journalists, for critical discussion. Nierenberg's nutrient-rich, versatile ratatouille-inspired recipe uses "imperfect" produce from the overlap of the summer and fall growing seasons, and pairs well with pasta, rice or crusty bread. As she cheekily notes in her recipe, it is a perfect dish for making the most of any produce you have neglected in the garden or refrigerator, thus cutting back on food waste. This version is vegan, but feel free to sprinkle on grated cheese if you are so inclined.

Preheat the oven to 350°F (180°C).

Cut the large imperfect tomatoes into chunks and place in a medium bowl. Use the back of a wooden spoon to smash the tomatoes until crushed. Add the garlic, ¼ cup (60 ml) of the olive oil and the cayenne pepper. Season generously with salt and pepper and stir to combine. Spread the tomato sauce on the bottom of a 9 x 13-inch (23 by 33 cm) or similar-sized glass or metal baking dish.

Arrange the sliced tomatoes, bell peppers, eggplants, zucchini and red onion upright in an alternating pattern in tight rows to fill the entire baking dish. Drizzle with the remaining ¼ cup (60 ml) of olive oil, sprinkle with the rosemary and season with salt and pepper. Bake until the vegetables are completely soft and tender, about 2 hours and 30 minutes. Finish with the rosemary sprig and serve with pasta, rice or crusty bread.

2 large imperfect tomatoes, plus 4 medium bruised tomatoes, cut into ¼-inch-thick (0.5 cm) slices

4 bruised garlic cloves, minced

½ cup (120 ml) olive oil

1 teaspoon cayenne pepper

Salt and freshly ground black pepper

4 small end-of-season red or green bell peppers, sliced crosswise into ¼-inch-thick (0.5) rings

3 baby eggplants, cut into ¼-inch-thick (0.5 cm) slices

2 medium zucchini that are looking a little tired, cut into ¼-inch-thick (0.5 cm) slices

2 medium red onions on their last legs, cut into ¼-inch-thick (0.5 cm) rings

2 teaspoons fresh rosemary that has been in your refrigerator far too long and needs to be used, finely chopped, plus a rosemary sprig for serving

Rice, couscous, pasta or crusty bread, for serving

MUURINPOHJALETTU
Large Griddle Pancake

Kati Partanen
Finland

Yield: 4 to 6 servings
Active time: 1 hour and 30 minutes
Total time: 2 hours

For the pancakes:

4 ½ cups (1.1 liters) whole milk

3 sustainably sourced large eggs

1 cup (125 g) barley flour

1 cup (120 g) whole wheat flour

1 ½ teaspoons salt

Unsalted butter, for cooking

For the filling:

¼ cup (60 ml) olive oil

3 medium carrots, peeled and diced

2 medium parsnips, peeled and diced

1 red bell pepper, diced

1 yellow bell pepper, diced

1 small white onion, diced

3 garlic cloves, finely chopped

5 ½ ounces (154 g) crème fraîche or cream cheese

1 tablespoon fresh lemon juice

Salt and freshly ground black pepper

Fresh herbs, such as parsley, basil or chives

Farmer Kati Partanen from Iisalmi, Finland, is a board member of the Finnish Farmer Union MTK and chair of the Women's Committee at the World Farmers' Organization. She advocates for fair revenue distribution across the food chain and renewed respect for ingredients in order to produce better food and less waste. Muurinpohjalettu were traditionally cooked on large pots still hot from doing the laundry in them and made with barley and wheat flours, two grains cultivated regionally. They are a great way to limit food waste: Partanen says that you can use just about any leftover vegetables, including ones that are wilting a bit, and even milk that is starting to sour (at your discretion). You can also make these with sweet fillings, such as jam. Partanen says these are always a hit with children.

Make the pancake batter:

In a large bowl, whisk together the milk, eggs, barley flour, whole wheat flour and salt until fully combined. Let stand for 1 hour. The goal is to have very thin, crispy pancakes, so the batter should be very thin.

While the batter rests, make the filling:

In a large frying pan, heat the olive oil over medium-high heat. Add the carrots, parsnips, bell peppers, onion and garlic and cook, stirring, until tender, 10 to 12 minutes. Reduce the heat to low, add the crème fraîche and stir to combine. Remove from the heat, add the lemon juice and season with salt and pepper. Sprinkle with herbs, reserving some for serving, and keep warm. (If the mixture seizes while it stands, place over low heat, add a splash of water and stir to loosen it.)

Cook the pancakes:

Set a sheet pan in the oven and preheat the oven to 250°F (125°C).

In a large (at least 8-inch / 20 cm) cast-iron frying pan, melt 1 teaspoon of butter over medium heat. Once the butter stops bubbling, stir the batter then add about ⅓ cup (75 ml) and swirl or tilt the pan to spread the batter and completely cover the bottom of the pan. Cook until the bottom is golden brown, about 1 minute. Using a spatula, carefully flip the pancake over and cook until the other side is golden brown, about 30 seconds. Transfer to the oven to keep warm, stacking as you make more pancakes. Continue cooking pancakes, occasionally whisking the batter and adding more butter to the pan as needed.

Spread filling on one half of a pancake. Fold the other half over the filling and then roll up for serving. Repeat with the remaining filling and pancakes, sprinkle with fresh herbs and serve warm.

KELOR MESANTEN

I Putu Dodik Sumarjana
Indonesia

Yield: 4 servings
Active time: 2 hours
Total time: 2 hours

I Putu Dodik Sumarjana is an Indonesian chef who is passionate about food and its role in our lives. He believes there is life in every food we eat and that each dish we create expresses beautiful stories that dance between taste and sensation. Within Indonesia, there has been a rapid rise in meat consumption alongside an increase of people facing extreme hunger. Sumarjana creates his dishes with all locally sourced ingredients, including kelor, which is native to Indonesia. Also known as moringa, kelor is a nutritious plant that is used as an herbal medicine around the world and is a good source of protein, as well as vitamins A, B and C. Sumarjana's recipe demonstrates an exciting new way we can use foods like kelor to improve our health, while also helping the planet. Traditionally, this dish utilized rescued coconuts that would have otherwise gone to waste. To make it at home, seek out young green coconuts that are unpeeled, exactly like they come off the tree. Alternatively, you can use white young coconuts. Bongkot is also called ginger torch and is available at Asian markets, but galangal or ginger can be used in its place. If you are unable to find kelor, use spinach, collard greens or Swiss chard.

Using a very sharp knife, carefully cut off just enough of the bottom of each coconut to allow them to sit flat on a grill. Next, use a cleaver and a rubber mallet or hammer to cut a slice off the top of each coconut, then drain the coconut water. Set the coconut water aside. Using the cleaver and rubber mallet or hammer, carefully and as neatly as possible cut off the top one-quarter of each coconut. You will use the bottom three-quarters of each coconut as serving bowls. Drain off and reserve any remaining coconut water.

Continue cutting the meat away from the coconut to create a bowl. Pour about half of the coconut water back into the coconuts. Reserve the rest for another use (or simply drink it with a slice of lime and some ice cubes). Return about half of the coconut meat to the coconuts. Set the filled coconut bowls aside while you make the rest of the soup.

Preheat a grill to medium-high (400 to 450°F / 200 to 230°C).

In a medium saucepan, warm the coconut oil over medium heat. Add the base genep and makrut lime leaves and sauté until fragrant, about 3 minutes. Remove from the heat, add the bongkot, kelor leaves and coconut milk. Place the pan back over medium heat and cook, stirring, until the kelor leaves are wilted and tender, 2 to 4 minutes. Season with salt. Keep warm while you grill the coconuts.

Place the coconut bottoms directly on the grill rack, cover and cook until the outside is roasted and the inside is very hot, about 15 minutes. Carefully remove the coconuts from the grill, then divide the kelor-coconut milk mixture between them. Serve in the center of the table so everyone can help themselves, making sure to scrape coconut meat into their bowls.

BASE GENEP

Yield: Makes about ¾ cup (140 g); active time: 45 minutes; total time: 45 minutes

In a food processor, grind the coriander seeds, white and black peppercorns, cloves and nutmeg until finely ground. Add the shallot, garlic, ginger, galangal, turmeric and chilis and grind into a grainy pulp.

For the 2 young green coconuts:

¼ cup (60 ml) coconut oil

¾ cup (140 g) base genep (recipe follows)

4 fresh or frozen makrut lime leaves

4 (1-inch) pieces fresh or frozen bongkot, sliced

7 ounces (200 g) fresh or frozen kelor (moringa) leaves

¼ cup (60 ml) coconut milk, or more to taste

Salt

For the Base Genep:

4 coriander seeds

2 white peppercorns

1 black peppercorn

¼ teaspoon ground cloves

¼ teaspoon freshly grated nutmeg

1 small shallot, finely chopped

1 small head garlic, cloves separated and finely chopped

2 (1-inch / 2.5 cm) pieces ginger, peeled and finely chopped

1 (1-inch / 2.5 cm) piece galangal, peeled and finely chopped

1 (2-inch / 5 cm) piece turmeric, peeled and finely chopped

2 to 3 fresh cayenne chilis, finely chopped

IJJEH
Zucchini Herb Fritters

Omayah Atassi
Syria

Yield: 6 to 8 servings
Active time: 40 minutes
Total time: 1 hour

4 bunches fresh flat-leaf parsley, leaves picked off and chopped

2 medium zucchini (about 9 ounces / 252 g each), coarsely grated

2 medium russet potatoes (about ½ pound / 225 g each), coarsely grated

½ bunch fresh mint, leaves picked off and chopped

Salt and freshly ground black pepper

8 sustainably sourced large eggs, beaten

⅔ cup (85 g) all-purpose flour

1 tablespoon ground cumin

2 to 3 teaspoons Aleppo pepper flakes (optional)

3 cups (720 ml) canola oil, for frying

Yogurt or labneh (strained yogurt), for serving

Omayah Atassi is a Syrian home cook who works to collect traditional family recipes that are verbally passed down from one generation to the next. Atassi notes that while the written word may eliminate some of the touch, feel and smell that comes with learning from our elders, it allows for those living in diaspora to learn the habits and tastes of their homeland. Although years of war and rising poverty have limited the amount and quality of accessible foods in Syria, traditional Syrian cooking is natural, health-promoting and sustainable, ensuring waste is reduced and promoting the availability of delicious food year round. Focusing on seasonal, locally sourced, plant-based ingredients, these fritters, known as Ijjeh in Syria, are a low-waste, nutritious and flavor-packed vegetarian meal, customarily enjoyed as an appetizer or for breakfast, as well as for iftar, the breaking of the fast meal during Ramadan.

Set aside a small handful of the parsley for garnish. In a large colander set in the sink, combine the remaining parsley with the zucchini, potatoes and mint. Sprinkle with 2 teaspoons of salt and use your hands to mix well, squeezing the vegetables and herbs a bit. Let drain for about 30 minutes. Press down on the vegetables and herbs to release their juices, then place in a clean kitchen towel and squeeze, twisting the towel as needed, until no liquid drips out. Place in a large bowl. Add the eggs, flour, cumin, ½ teaspoon black pepper and the Aleppo pepper, if using, and stir to combine.

Fill a large, deep skillet with enough canola oil to come about ½ inch (1.25 cm) up the side. Place over medium-high heat and bring to 350°F (180°C) on a deep-fry thermometer.

Preheat the oven to 250°F (125°C). Line a sheet pan with a rack and place in the oven. Line a second sheet pan with paper towels and set near the stove.

Test the seasoning of the fritter mixture by frying a small dollop. Adjust seasoning as needed.

Scoop a scant ¼ cup (38 g) of the batter, then carefully drop it into the oil and use a spatula to gently press it into a roughly 3-inch (7.5 cm) round fritter. Repeat to make two more fritters and fry, flipping once, until puffy and browned all over and cooked through, about 2 minutes per side. Transfer the fritters to the paper towel–lined sheet pan to drain, then set on the rack-lined sheet pan in the oven to keep warm. Continue frying fritters, adjusting the heat as needed to keep the oil at 350°F (180°C).

Sprinkle the fritters with the reserved parsley and serve warm with yogurt or labneh on the side.

GARBANZOS CON ESPINACAS
Moorish-Style Chickpea and Spinach Stew

José Andrés
Spain

Yield: 4 servings
Active time: 25 minutes
Total time: 35 minutes

Spanish chef and activist José Andrés founded World Central Kitchen, a non-profit organization that delivers food relief in the wake of natural and humanitarian disasters. Through his work, Andrés unites chefs around the world to contribute to a better food system, always considering regional cuisines and preferences when supporting local communities. Andrés' passion for sustainable ingredients is demonstrated in this recipe that uses both canned chickpeas and their liquid to reduce food waste and create a robust stew, best enjoyed with crusty bread.

¼ cup (60 ml) extra-virgin olive oil, preferably Spanish

6 garlic cloves, peeled

2 ounces (56 g) sliced white bread, crusts removed (1 to 2 slices)

2 tablespoons pimentón

1 pinch saffron threads, preferably Spanish

1 teaspoon ground cumin

2 tablespoons sherry vinegar

2 (14-ounce / 400 g) cans chickpeas (do not drain)

½ pound (225 g) spinach

Kosher salt and freshly ground white pepper

Crusty bread, for serving

In a small frying pan, heat the oil over medium-low heat. Add the garlic and cook, stirring, until browned, about 3 minutes. Remove the garlic from the pan and set it aside. Working in batches as needed, add the bread to the pan and brown it on both sides, about 1 minute per side. Remove the bread from the pan and set it aside. Do not clean the pan.

Using a mortar and pestle, smash the browned garlic and toasted bread into a very thick paste.

Once the pan used to cook the garlic and bread has cooled for a few minutes, add the pimentón, saffron and cumin, followed by the sherry vinegar. Stir to combine and set the pan aside.

In a medium saucepan, bring the chickpeas and their liquid to a low boil over medium heat. Add the spinach and a little water as needed if there's not enough liquid to cook the spinach. Simmer for 5 minutes and then add the pimentón mixture, along with the garlic-bread paste, and stir to combine—you should have a thick, stew-like sauce.

Continue simmering until the chickpeas are soft and flavorful, about 5 more minutes. Season with salt and white pepper and serve hot with crusty bread.

Julius Roberts
England

Massimo Bottura
Italy

Saliha Bala
Kabylic community
Algeria

Ursula Schersch
Austria

Niven Patel
India

Sotha Sok
Cambodia

Adrian Hădean
Romania

Eelke Plasmeijer
The Netherlands

Jamsel Gyaltshen
Bhutan

Lisa Johnson
Antarctica

Danielle Nierenberg
United States

Kati Partanen
Finland

I Putu Dodik
Sumarjana
Indonesia

Omayah Atassi
Syria

José Andrés
Spain

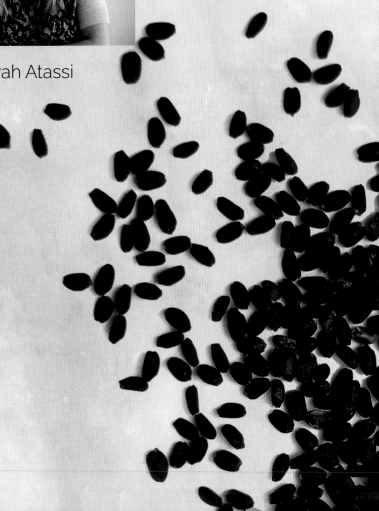

Components of Our Food

CARBOHYDRATES

Carbohydrates are the main fuel source for our brain and muscles. While carbohydrates are an important part of our diet, not all carbohydrates offer the same nutrient density—some have more health benefits than others. We can determine the total carbohydrates on a food label by adding the grams of the sugar and fiber in the food item.

CARBOHYDRATES ARE FOUND IN A VARIETY OF DIFFERENT FOODS:

- Fruits and starchy vegetables, such as bananas, apples, potatoes and corn
  - » Fruits and vegetables are high in fiber and rich in antioxidants, vitamins and minerals that help us feel energized and can help to prevent chronic disease.
- Grains, such as rice, breads, pastas and cereals
  - » It is best for us to choose whole or intact grains instead of refined grains (for example, we should choose brown rice over white rice) to reap the benefits of their higher fiber content.
- Legumes, such as lentils and chickpeas
  - » Legumes like black beans, chickpeas and lentils provide heart-healthy fiber and gut-friendly resistant starch. They are also a good source of plant-based protein.
- Dairy products, such as milk, milk products, yogurt and cheese
  - » Many dairy products are fortified with vitamins A and D. Fortification refers to the process of adding vitamins and minerals to a food to increase its nutrients.
  - » Milk-based dairy protein is a complete protein, meaning it contains all nine essential amino acids (protein building blocks) that our bodies cannot produce and therefore need to acquire through food. Dairy foods can be full-fat (4%), reduced-fat (2%), low-fat (1%) or non-fat (0%).
- Sweets and sugary beverages, such as candies, ice cream, cakes, jam, juices, soda and sports drinks.
  - » These choices do not offer the antioxidants and fiber that whole food carbohydrate sources do. Eating too many of them might leave little room for healthier foods.

PROTEIN

Protein is essential for the growth and development of healthy muscles and tissues, supporting our immune health and aiding in wound healing. Like carbohydrates, not all sources of protein are created equally. "High quality" proteins traditionally refer to proteins sourced from animals because they contain all nine essential amino acids that keep our bodies functioning optimally. However, protein can also be found in a variety of plant-based foods.

- Sustainable animal sources include chicken, fish and shellfish, cage-free eggs, grass-fed beef, turkey, game meats and whey protein powder.
- Plant-based sources include lentils, beans, quinoa, chia seeds, tofu, tempeh, seitan and pea protein powder.

HEALTHY FATS

Fats are essential for our bodies to produce hormones, absorb vitamins and stay full. Certain fats promote good health, while others can lead to poor health and disease. Sources of healthy fats include avocado, olives and olive oil, ghee, nuts, seeds, cheese, yogurt and coconut. These fats are considered "healthy" because they are mostly monounsaturated and polyunsaturated fats, which lower cholesterol and triglycerides, and can reduce your risk of heart disease.

- Monounsaturated: olive oil, peanut oil, canola oil, avocados, most nuts, high-oleic safflower and sunflower oils.
- Polyunsaturated: There are two main types of polyunsaturated fats: omega-3 fatty acids and omega-6 fatty acids. Omega-3 fatty acids are especially important to prioritize.
  » Omega-6 fatty acids are found in vegetable oils, such as safflower, soybean, sunflower, walnut and corn oils.
  » Omega-3 fatty acids are found in fatty fish, such as salmon, mackerel and sardines, as well as flaxseeds, walnuts, canola oil and unhydrogenated soybean oil.
- It is best to avoid foods high in saturated and trans fat. Foods high in these kinds of fat are often found in fast, fried or packaged foods. Saturated fats do not directly raise blood sugar levels, but they have been linked to increased inflammation, insulin resistance, lower HDL (good) cholesterol levels and impaired heart function.
  » Foods high in saturated fat to be consumed in moderation include high-fat dairy products, high-fat meat products like bacon, creamy sauces, lards, tropical oils and butters.
- Similar to saturated fat, trans fat increases LDL (bad) blood cholesterol levels. Trans fat does not occur in nature and is the least health-supportive fat—try avoiding it as much as possible in favor of mono and polyunsaturated options.
  » Foods high in trans fats include processed snacks (crackers, crisps and chips), shelf-stable baked goods (muffins, cookies and cakes), frozen meals, fast foods, coffee creamers, refrigerated dough products and foods made with or cooked in hydrogenated oils. Choose foods that either do not contain hydrogenated oil or where a liquid oil is listed first in the ingredient list.

SODIUM

Diets high in sodium can lead to high blood pressure, which contributes to health conditions like heart disease. Processed meats and cheeses, canned and frozen foods, packaged foods and seasonings/sauces are often high in sodium.

ADDED SUGAR

Diets high in added sugar can result in insulin resistance, increased inflammation and type 2 diabetes. Added sugar has many names, which makes it hard to find on an ingredient label. There are more than 25 different names for sugar approved for labeling use! These include common names, such as sucrose and high-fructose corn syrup, but also barley, malt, dextrose, maltose and rice syrup. A good rule of thumb is if the word ends in "-ose" (examples: fructose, sucrose, maltose, dextrose), it signifies added sugar.

FIBER

Fiber is important because it helps us feel fuller for longer and promotes good gut health. By supporting digestion and nutrient absorption, fiber helps manage blood sugar spikes after meals, leading to more stable energy levels and fewer dramatic cravings. Fiber is only found in plant foods, such as fruits, vegetables, whole grains, seeds and nuts. Fiber is indigestible, so it does not provide any calories!

MEASURING

The shortcuts below can be "handy" measuring tools when deciding how much food to cook and serve. Of course, portions should be tailored to each person's unique needs!

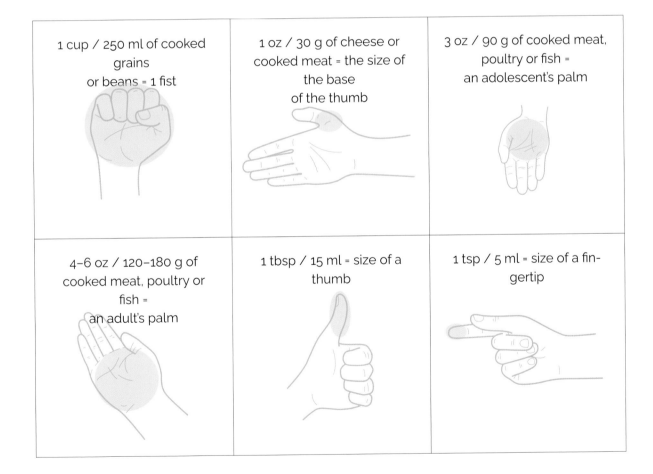

| 1 cup / 250 ml of cooked grains or beans = 1 fist | 1 oz / 30 g of cheese or cooked meat = the size of the base of the thumb | 3 oz / 90 g of cooked meat, poultry or fish = an adolescent's palm |
| 4–6 oz / 120–180 g of cooked meat, poultry or fish = an adult's palm | 1 tbsp / 15 ml = size of a thumb | 1 tsp / 5 ml = size of a fingertip |

Nutrition Labeling Methodology

The ESHA Food Processor software was utilized for this cookbook to provide a dietary analysis of each recipe. Food Processor is an extensively researched food and nutrition database of more than 100,000 foods and food items, including common foods, restaurant items, ingredients and recipes. The estimates include total calories and grams of fat, carbohydrate, sodium, sugar, fiber and protein in each recipe. All of the calculations are approximations, as international research agencies typically allow for a 20 percent discrepancy on the nutrition facts panel.

FOOD LABEL TIPS & TRICKS

Various international scientific organizations have developed helpful tools for consumers to navigate the food we eat and to interpret nutrition labels. Using a nutrition facts label is one of many ways we can help ourselves and our family and friends to make health-supportive food choices that meet our daily needs. Eating too many calories can increase risk factors associated with various chronic diseases like diabetes, hypertension and cardiovascular disease, while eating too few can leave us under-energized or ill. It is important to also understand that calories are not created equal—certain foods provide more nutrients than others despite containing the same number of calories. We can optimize our health by eating foods that are both rich in nutrients and hit the "sweet spot" of our caloric, or energy, needs. Here are some daily intake goals to keep in mind, according to the Food and Agriculture Organization of the United Nations and the World Health Organization:

- Fat: Maintain a total fat intake of 30 percent or less of total energy intake to support cognitive health and vitamin absorption.
  - » Saturated fat: Ideally, no more than 10 percent of total energy intake comes from saturated fat. Foods with 1 gram or less saturated fat per serving are considered "low in saturated fat."
  - » Trans fat: It is best to minimize trans fat as much as possible, so that it accounts for 1 percent or less of our total energy intake.
- Sodium: The World Health Organization recommends an intake of no more than 5 added grams of iodized salt per day. If a food has more than 300 milligrams (mg) sodium per serving, it is a high-sodium food. Sodium might also be labeled as salt, baking soda, baking powder, monosodium glutamate (MSG) or disodium phosphate on the ingredient label.
- Sugar: In both adults and children, added sugars should be reduced to less than 10 percent of total energy intake. A reduction to less than 5 percent of total energy intake would provide additional health benefits.
- Fiber: Women should target 25 g or more of fiber each day, and men should aim for 38 g or more fiber per day. Look for nutrition labels that have at least 3 g of fiber per serving, and prioritize whole fruits and vegetables.

Recipe Nutrition Information

 VEGAN   VEGETARIAN   PESCATARIAN

I. THE FOOD SYSTEM

1) SAFFRON CHICKEN WITH FREEKEH

Total Calories: 590 Grams of Fat: 19g Sodium: 220mg Total Carbohydrates: 58g Sugar: 7g Fiber: 12g Protein: 49g

2) CEDAR-PLANKED ARCTIC CHAR WITH GRILLED VEGETABLES

Total Calories: 330 Grams of Fat: 20g Sodium: 320mg Total Carbohydrates: 21g Sugar: 7g Fiber: 5g Protein: 23g

3) RED KIDNEY BEANS AND RICE CURRY

Total Calories: 570 Grams of Fat: 13g Sodium: 270mg Total Carbohydrates: 89g Sugar: 6g Fiber: 23g Protein: 29g

4) THE ZIMMERN FAMILY MATZO BALL SOUP

Total Calories: 370 Grams of Fat: 16g Sodium: 1310mg Total Carbohydrates: 20g Sugar: 1g Fiber: 0g Protein: 33g

5) MORINGA PESTO PASTA

Total Calories: 1020 Grams of Fat: 58g Sodium: 720mg Total Carbohydrates: 106g Sugar: 8g Fiber: 7g Protein: 26g

6) SOUPE PAYSANNE (SOUP JADEN—RED CABBAGE, YAM, GREEN PEAS AND SPINACH SOUP)

Total Calories: 280 Grams of Fat: 9g Sodium: 460mg Total Carbohydrates: 47g Sugar: 13g Fiber: 7g Protein: 7g

7) TALKAN

Total Calories: 130 Grams of Fat: 7g Sodium: 0mg Total Carbohydrates: 16g Sugar: 5g Fiber: 2g Protein: 2g

8) APPLE CRANBERRY PECAN WILD RICE PILAF

Total Calories: 300 Grams of Fat: 10g Sodium: 150mg Total Carbohydrates: 48g Sugar: 22g Fiber: 4g Protein: 7g

9) PEPPER-BRAISED FISH

Total Calories: 300 Grams of Fat: 20g Sodium: 150mg Total Carbohydrates: 6g Sugar: 3g Fiber: 3g Protein: 22g

10) SALATAT BAZINJAN (AUBERGINE SALAD)

Total Calories: 420 Grams of Fat: 38g Sodium: 45mg Total Carbohydrates: 18g Sugar: 9g Fiber: 8g Protein: 5g

11) KUNA FISH AND VEGETABLE STEW

Total Calories: 650 Grams of Fat: 26g Sodium: 340mg Total Carbohydrates: 73g Sugar: 13g Fiber: 2g Protein: 34g

12) SPIRULINA-TOSSED VEGETABLE SALAD

Total Calories: 180 Grams of Fat: 2g Sodium: 370mg Total Carbohydrates: 33g Sugar: 8g Fiber: 7g Protein: 9g

13) ENKUM

Total Calories: 420 Grams of Fat: 7g Sodium: 20mg Total Carbohydrates: 85g Sugar: 14g Fiber: 9g Protein: 12g

14) PESCADO CON PATACONES (FISH AND FRIED GREEN PLANTAINS)

Total Calories: 650 Grams of Fat: 37g Sodium: 100mg Total Carbohydrates: 58g Sugar: 27g Fiber: 4g Protein: 31g

15) ONION-POACHED MACKEREL WITH OKRA AND RED BELL PEPPERS

Total Calories: 220 Grams of Fat: 12g Sodium: 50mg Total Carbohydrates: 16g Sugar: 6g Fiber: 5g Protein: 14g

II. BIODIVERSITY

1) STINGING NETTLE TART WITH BREADNUT OLIVE OIL CRUST

Total Calories: 210 Grams of Fat: 14g Sodium: 440mg Total Carbohydrates: 14g Sugar: 2g Fiber: 2g Protein: 7g

2) BAKED SALMON WITH SUMAC, FENNEL AND FIGS

Total Calories: 620 Grams of Fat: 35g Sodium: 210mg Total Carbohydrates: 21g Sugar: 14g Fiber: 7g Protein: 54g

3) VENISON CARPACCIO WITH WATERCRESS SALAD

Total Calories: 570 Grams of Fat: 43g Sodium: 180mg Total Carbohydrates: 9g Sugar: 1g Fiber: 5g Protein: 42g

4) ADOBO BREADFRUIT WITH PICO DE GALLO

Total Calories: 110 Grams of Fat: 2.5g Sodium: 180mg Total Carbohydrates: 24g Sugar: 12g Fiber: 5g Protein: 3g

5) NASI ULAM (VEGAN RICE SALAD WITH HOMEGROWN HERBS)

Total Calories: 360 Grams of Fat: 11g Sodium: 15mg Total Carbohydrates: 59g Sugar: 2g Fiber: 2g Protein: 7g

6) SEAFOOD OKRA

Total Calories: 260 Grams of Fat: 8g Sodium: 460mg Total Carbohydrates: 15g Sugar: 4g Fiber: 5g Protein: 32g

7) SUSHI SALAAM

Total Calories: 540 Grams of Fat: 31g Sodium: 250mg Total Carbohydrates: 59g Sugar: 11g Fiber: 12g Protein: 12g

8) MORINGA TEFF LASAGNA

Total Calories: 550 Grams of Fat: 19g Sodium: 960mg Total Carbohydrates: 70g Sugar: 8g Fiber: 8g Protein: 26g

9) FRESH TUNA SALAD WITH HARISSA VINAIGRETTE

Total Calories: 410 Grams of Fat: 20g Sodium: 1320mg Total Carbohydrates: 26g Sugar: 5g Fiber: 4g Protein: 30g

10) SPICY OLLUCO WITH BEEF

Total Calories: 330 Grams of Fat: 15g Sodium: 490mg Total Carbohydrates: 27g Sugar: 3g Fiber: 3g Protein: 18g

11) BUTTERNUT SQUASH LOCRO WITH QUINOA AND BRAZIL NUT CRUMBLE

Total Calories: 970 Grams of Fat: 58g Sodium: 1970mg Total Carbohydrates: 88g Sugar: 20g Fiber: 16g Protein: 27g

12) FONIO AND SWEET POTATO CRAB CAKES WITH SPICY PAPAYA-LIME SAUCE

Total Calories: 280 Grams of Fat: 9g Sodium: 620mg Total Carbohydrates: 35g Sugar: 3g Fiber: 3g Protein: 16g

13) SQUID WITH TOMATOES

Total Calories: 180 Grams of Fat: 10g Sodium: 50mg Total Carbohydrates: 8g Sugar: 3g Fiber: 1g Protein: 15g

14) PAPEDA (SAGO PASTE) WITH FISH AND VEGETABLES

Total Calories: 560 Grams of Fat: 35g Sodium: 410mg Total Carbohydrates: 46g Sugar: 12g Fiber: 4g Protein: 22g

15) CASHEW-CRUSTED FISH WITH CARAMBOLA SAUCE

Total Calories: 260 Grams of Fat: 15g Sodium: 60mg Total Carbohydrates: 23g Sugar: 16g Fiber: 2g Protein: 9g

III. SUSTAINABLE CONSUMPTION

1) PLANTAIN PURÉE

Total Calories: 190 Grams of Fat: 4.5g Sodium: 5mg Total Carbohydrates: 40g Sugar: 19g Fiber: 3g Protein: 2g

2) CHORBA WITH ROASTED EGGPLANT AND SWEET POTATOES

Total Calories: 290 Grams of Fat: 8g Sodium: 510mg Total Carbohydrates: 49g Sugar: 13g Fiber: 9g Protein: 8g

3) SWEET POTATO GNOCCHI WITH KALE AND WALNUT BASIL PESTO

Total Calories: 700 Grams of Fat: 29g Sodium: 1270mg Total Carbohydrates: 100g Sugar: 18g Fiber: 16g Protein: 14g

4) KADOO (AFGHAN BRAISED SQUASH WITH GARLICKY YOGURT SAUCE)

Total Calories: 310 Grams of Fat: 12g Sodium: 200mg Total Carbohydrates: 47g Sugar: 21g Fiber: 7g Protein: 10g

5) TOM KHA (GALANGAL SOUP WITH TOFU AND MUSHROOMS)

Total Calories: 490 Grams of Fat: 35g Sodium: 1740mg Total Carbohydrates: 20g Sugar: 11g Fiber: 1g Protein: 25g

6) TANGERINE AND TURMERIC BRAZILIAN CHICKEN STEW

Total Calories: 210 Grams of Fat: 14g Sodium: 60mg Total Carbohydrates: 13g Sugar: 6g Fiber: 3g Protein: 11g

7) RED LENTILS AND BULGUR (MJADRA HAMRA)

Total Calories: 450 Grams of Fat: 14g Sodium: 10mg Total Carbohydrates: 65g Sugar: 3g Fiber: 11g Protein: 19g

8) SPANAKOPITA

Total Calories: 560 Grams of Fat: 37g Sodium: 860mg Total Carbohydrates: 44g Sugar: 4g Fiber: 3g Protein: 17g

9) BEAN AND BELL PEPPER CHILI WITH CAULIFLOWER RICE

Total Calories: 420 Grams of Fat: 15g Sodium: 840mg Total Carbohydrates: 59g Sugar: 13g Fiber: 18g Protein: 19g

10) SCALLION TARTE TATIN

Total Calories: 390 Grams of Fat: 25g Sodium: 220mg Total Carbohydrates: 35g Sugar: 11g Fiber: 3g Protein: 6g

11) SOPA DE MILHO (BRAZILIAN CORN CHOWDER)

Total Calories: 320 Grams of Fat: 12g Sodium: 210mg Total Carbohydrates: 50g Sugar: 10g Fiber: 7g Protein: 9g

12) KERA NA CUTLETS (BANANA CROQUETTES WITH AMARANTH)

Total Calories: 630 Grams of Fat: 57g Sodium: 10mg Total Carbohydrates: 30g Sugar: 2g Fiber: 2g Protein: 4g

13) SHULBATO (COOKED BULGUR WITH EGGPLANT, PEPPERS AND TOMATOES)

Total Calories: 610 Grams of Fat: 34g Sodium: 260mg Total Carbohydrates: 72g Sugar: 14g Fiber: 16g Protein: 14g

14) SOPA DE LIMA (YUCATAN LIME SOUP)

Total Calories: 140 Grams of Fat: 8g Sodium: 270mg Total Carbohydrates: 5g Sugar: 1g Fiber: 1g Protein: 12g

15) SOUTH AFRICAN BOBOTIE

Total Calories: 630 Grams of Fat: 29g Sodium: 210mg Total Carbohydrates: 66g Sugar: 20g Fiber: 6g Protein: 28g

IV. FOOD & CLIMATE CHANGE

1) ON SIKIL BI BU'UL (BLACK BEAN PIPIAN)

Total Calories: 90 Grams of Fat: 1g Sodium: 360mg Total Carbohydrates: 16g Sugar: 0g Fiber: 6g Protein: 6g kg CO_2e: 0.04

2) SWEET AND SOUR PUMPKIN

Total Calories: 260 Grams of Fat: 17g Sodium: 5mg Total Carbohydrates: 29g Sugar: 14g Fiber: 8g Protein: 4g (kg CO_2e): 0.05

3) WHITE TEPARY BEANS AND NOPALES SALAD

Total Calories: 260 Grams of Fat: 6g Sodium: 370mg Total Carbohydrates: 42g Sugar: 10g Fiber: 9g Protein: 12g (kg CO_2e): 0.06

4) BULGUR AND SPINACH WITH YOGURT AND POMEGRANATE

Total Calories: 200 Grams of Fat: 8g Sodium: 350mg Total Carbohydrates: 31g Sugar: 8g Fiber: 6g Protein: 4g (kg CO_2e): 0.07

5) BRAISED CUT KOMBU WITH MUSHROOMS AND SHIRATAKI

Total Calories: 100 Grams of Fat: 2.5g Sodium: 1230mg Total Carbohydrates: 15g Sugar: 6g Fiber: 6g Protein: 3g (kg CO_2e): 0.08

6) "LA BANDERA" DOMINICANA (DOMINICAN RICE AND BEANS)

Total Calories: 280 Grams of Fat: 7g Sodium: 1250mg Total Carbohydrates: 49g Sugar: 2g Fiber: 4g Protein: 8g (kg CO_2e): 0.11

7) SHORBAT ADDAS (MAMA'S LENTIL SOUP)

Total Calories: 240 Grams of Fat: 11g Sodium: 35mg Total Carbohydrates: 30g Sugar: 2g Fiber: 5g Protein: 9g (kg CO_2e): 0.11

8) VEGGIE STICK SALAD WITH DRAGON FRUIT AND STAR FRUIT

Total Calories: 140 Grams of Fat: 2.5g Sodium: 100mg Total Carbohydrates: 25g Sugar: 16g Fiber: 6g Protein: 5g (kg CO2e): 0.12

9) DANDELION SALAD TOWER WITH SORGHUM FLOUR FLATBREAD AND HONEY-CITRUS VINAIGRETTE

Total Calories: 440 Grams of Fat: 16g Sodium: 310mg Total Carbohydrates: 71g Sugar: 22g Fiber: 6g Protein: 8g (kg CO2e): 0.13

10) WHITE BEANS WITH CHAYOTE AND SPINACH

Total Calories: 90 Grams of Fat: 0g Sodium: 115mg Total Carbohydrates: 28g Sugar: 11g Fiber: 3g Protein: 1g (kg CO2e): 0.13

11) GREEN BANANA CEVICHE

Total Calories: 90 Grams of Fat: 0g Sodium: 115mg Total Carbohydrates: 28g Sugar: 11g Fiber: 3g Protein: 1g (kg CO2e): 0.14

12) HAWAIIAN GREENS WITH SWEET POTATOES

Total Calories: 100 Grams of Fat: 2.5g Sodium: 290mg Total Carbohydrates: 17g Sugar: 4g Fiber: 3g Protein: 3g (kg CO2e): 0.14

13) MUSHROOM "BULGOGI" SSAMBAP WITH SPICY SSAM SAUCE

Total Calories: 200 Grams of Fat: 13g Sodium: 1170mg Total Carbohydrates: 18g Sugar: 11g Fiber: 6g Protein: 3g (kg CO2e): 0.15

14) APOTH NJUGU (JUTE MALLOW WITH PEANUT BUTTER)

Total Calories: 350 Grams of Fat: 26g Sodium: 530mg Total Carbohydrates: 18g Sugar: 6g Fiber: 7g Protein: 12g (kg CO2e): 0.16

15) SOUP JOUMOU

Total Calories: 260 Grams of Fat: 13g Sodium: 55mg Total Carbohydrates: 34g Sugar: 8g Fiber: 5g Protein: 5g (kg CO2e): 0.16

V. REDUCING FOOD WASTE

1) COCONUT AND TOMATO STEW

Total Calories: 280 Grams of Fat: 24g Sodium: 25mg Total Carbohydrates: 17g Sugar: 8g Fiber: 4g Protein: 5g

2) NONNA ANCELLA'S PASSATELLI

Total Calories: 180 Grams of Fat: 8g Sodium: 280mg Total Carbohydrates: 15g Sugar: 1g Fiber: 1g Protein: 11g

3) MUSHROOM BOUREK

Total Calories: 180 Grams of Fat: 14g Sodium: 270mg Total Carbohydrates: 11g Sugar: 2g Fiber: 1g Protein: 3g

4) ERDÄPFELGULASCH (AUSTRIAN-STYLE POTATO GOULASH)

Total Calories: 220 Grams of Fat: 8g Sodium: 580mg Total Carbohydrates: 36g Sugar: 4g Fiber: 4g Protein: 5g (kg CO2e): 0.23

5) CARROT BIRYANI

Total Calories: 310 Grams of Fat: 10g Sodium: 270mg Total Carbohydrates: 48g Sugar: 11g Fiber: 4g Protein: 8g

6) SAMLOR KORKO (CAMBODIAN STIRRING POT SOUP)

Total Calories: 180 Grams of Fat: 4.5g Sodium: 1820mg Total Carbohydrates: 26g Sugar: 12g Fiber: 2g Protein: 11g

7) CHARRED CABBAGE

Total Calories: 350 Grams of Fat: 34g Sodium: 55mg Total Carbohydrates: 11g Sugar: 6g Fiber: 4g Protein: 3g

8) PICCALILLI

Total Calories: 140 Grams of Fat: 0g Sodium: 1040mg Total Carbohydrates: 37g Sugar: 26g Fiber: 1g Protein: 1g

9) SHAMDEY

Total Calories: 450 Grams of Fat: 23g Sodium: 80mg Total Carbohydrates: 48g Sugar: 2g Fiber: 1g Protein: 11g

10) JOSEPHINE'S QUICHE LORRAINE

Total Calories: 350 Grams of Fat: 29g Sodium: 460mg Total Carbohydrates: 9g Sugar: 2g Fiber: 1g Protein: 14g

11) MAKE DO RATATOU(ILLE)

Total Calories: 300 Grams of Fat: 20g Sodium: 840mg Total Carbohydrates: 33g Sugar: 15g Fiber: 9g Protein: 5g

12) MUURINPOHJALETTU (LARGE GRIDDLE PANCAKE)

Total Calories: 540 Grams of Fat: 29g Sodium: 720mg Total Carbohydrates: 56g Sugar: 15g Fiber: 8g Protein: 17g

13) KELOR MESANTEN

Total Calories: 750 Grams of Fat: 70g Sodium: 45mg Total Carbohydrates: 34g Sugar: 13g Fiber: 19g Protein: 10g

14) IJJEH (ZUCCHINI HERB FRITTERS)

Total Calories: 340 Grams of Fat: 26g Sodium: 580mg Total Carbohydrates: 17g Sugar: 2g Fiber: 3g Protein: 10g

15) GARBANZOS CON ESPINACAS (MOORISH-STYLE CHICKPEA AND SPINACH STEW)

Total Calories: 370 Grams of Fat: 19g Sodium: 720mg Total Carbohydrates: 41g Sugar: 2g Fiber: 12g Protein: 14g

NOTES

- All calculations are for 1 serving of the total recipe yield.
- Each time salt was calculated, kosher salt was used.
- Sodium was not calculated for recipes calling for "salt and pepper to taste."
- For recipes that required frying, we used the standard 4 cups (960 ml) of oil. Depending on how porous the food is, 8–25 percent of the oil is absorbed during frying.
- Most international research organizations allow a 20 percent (!) discrepancy in calculations published on nutrition facts panels. We have tried our best to be as accurate as possible, but note that a margin for error remains.

About Kitchen Connection

THE KITCHEN CONNECTION ALLIANCE works in cooperation with the Food and Agriculture Organization of the United Nations and the United Nations Department of Global Communications to use food as a vehicle to connect people to each other, empowering global citizens to support a better food system for human and planetary health. This project is an extension of that mission.

 @kitchenconnection

About Familius

VISIT OUR WEBSITE: WWW.FAMILIUS.COM

Familius is a global trade publishing company that publishes books and other content to help families be happy. We believe that the family is the fundamental unit of society and that happy families are the foundation of a happy life. We recognize that every family looks different, and we passionately believe in helping all families find greater joy. To that end, we publish books for children and adults that invite families to live the Familius Ten Habits of Happy Family Life: *love together, play together, learn together, work together, talk together, heal together, read together, eat together, give together,* and *laugh together*. Founded in 2012, Familius is located in Sanger, California.

CONNECT

- Facebook: www.facebook.com/familiustalk
- Twitter: @familiustalk, @paterfamilius1
- Pinterest: www.pinterest.com/familius
- Instagram: @familiustalk

FAMILIUS

*The most important work you ever do
will be within the walls of your own home.*